Psychopathology: A Cognitive View

PSYCHOPATHOLOGY:
A COGNITIVE VIEW

ZVI GIORA, Ph.D.

TEL AVIV UNIVERSITY

GARDNER PRESS, INC.

NEW YORK

Distributed by Halsted Press
A Division of John Wiley & Sons, Inc.

NEW YORK • TORONTO • LONDON • SIDNEY

Gardner Press, Inc.
32 Washington Square West
New York, New York 10011

Distributed solely by the Halsted Press Division of John Wiley &
Sons, Inc., New York

Library of Congress Cataloging in Publication Data

Giora, Zvi
  Psychopathology: A cognitive view.

  Includes bibliographical references.
  1. Psychology, Pathological. I. Title.

  [DNLM: 1. Cognition. 2. Behavior. 3. Psychopathology.
  WM100 G497p]
  RC454.G56   616.8'9'07   75–17620

ISBN 0–470–30218–6

Printed in the United States of America
1 2 3 4 5 6 7 8 9

Contents

Chapter One

A Preview

THIS BOOK DELINEATES the cognitive approach to behavior in general and to psychopathology in particular. The psychodynamic approach is synonymous with the assumption that an analysis of behavior requires us to unveil the underlying unconscious motives. Motives, intentions, and will are, indeed, basic psychological concepts; and it is impossible to understand behavior without granting them proper consideration. However, motivation alone does not make behavior; there is no behavior without cognition. Nevertheless, many theories of personality and psychopathology suffer from a hypertrophy of the psychodynamical-motivational view and an insufficiency of the cognitive view. The time is ripe for a reorientation, which means for learning the real proportions between motives and the processes of cognition in shaping behavior.

A few years before Freud's *Psychopathology of Everyday Life* (1901), Meringer and Mayer (1895) published a study on slips of the tongue. Meringer's collection contains 4400 errors that occurred in natural speech, most of them produced by his colleagues at the University of Vienna. He also recorded the time of day the error occurred, the state of fatigue of the speaker, his estimated rate of speech at the time of the error, and the speaker's intuitions concerning the cause of his error. Since his colleagues were less than enthusiastic in pursuing this line of research, Meringer had to pay for his thoroughness by a growing unpopularity among his faculty mates. However, as McKay (1970) points out, Meringer has given us a study the extensiveness, validity, accuracy, and documentation of which are far superior to all other collections.

Meringer (and also Wundt) stressed a point which was to gain new respectability some fifty years later (Lashley, 1951)—that is, that what is to be uttered is anticipated, or rather, preprogrammed. McAdam and Whitaker (1971) were able to show that slow negative potentials, which are at a maximum over Broca's area in the left hemisphere, are generated when normal subjects spontaneously produce polysyllabic words. These potentials begin up to one second before word articulation. This preprogramming obviously can disturb, proactively and retroactively, the generation of words. For example, one of Meringer's subjects said: *"Es war mir auf der Schwest* [instead of *Brust*] *so schwer."* (It was so heavy on my breast.) *Brust* was apparently proactively disturbed by the preprogramming of *schwer* and the result was a hybrid: *Schwe-st.*

Freud (1901), on the other hand, emphasized motivation. Was what happened here, he wondered, simply that the sound *schwe* forced back the equally valent sound *bru* by anticipating it? "The idea can hardly be dismissed that the sounds making up *schwe* were further enabled to obtrude in this manner because of a special relation. That could only be the association *Schwester* (sister) and *Bruder* (brother); perhaps also *Brust der Schwester* (sister's breast), which leads one on to other groups of thoughts.

It is this invisible helper behind the scenes which lends the otherwise innocent *schwe* the strength to produce a mistake in speaking."

We have here before us many of the well-known ingredients characterizing Freud's reasoning: the innocent *schwe*, and the invisible helper behind the scenes combining in a new strength (cathexis) to obtrude and to produce a mistake. Also, it is rather clear that while acknowledging cognition, he assigned primacy to motivation. He was ready to agree that in situations where speaking is hurried and attention is to some extent diverted, the conditions governing slips of the tongue may easily be confined within the limits given by Meringer and Mayer. But, he added, in slips of the tongue collected by himself he was hardly able to find one example where these rules alone were enough to explain the disturbances. These slips arise "out of elements which are not intended to be uttered and of whose excitation we only learn precisely through the actual disturbance."

Freud's interpretation is conceivable, but even if his conjecture could be proven, that would not weaken the reasoning of Meringer, and also Wundt. In order to intrude, these alleged intentions had to undergo the same verbal processing as did the intruded sentence. To think of a sister's breast one has to think. To repeat: motivation alone does not make behavior, and there is no behavior without cognition. To speculate about which of them precedes the other one is like asking the question about the chicken or the egg. Viewed developmentally, though, the organs subserving a function must precede the emergence of the motive to fulfill this function. For instance, the organs of sexual reproduction precede the appearance of the sexual urge, but after that appears the wish and its control systems are necessarily interpenetrating processes.

In these days of revived interest and research in cognition, one does not risk much by such statements. Nevertheless, we do not possess as yet a systematic exposition of the role of cognition in psychopathology. That is what I venture to present here. The presentation mixes polemic with exposition. In the first chapters, which are polemical, I argue that it is not instinctual motives which lie at the base of behavior, but that we are fundamentally tuned to relate to our environment. I also point out the common eagerness to assume motives, even in instances where in fact the structural properties of information processing are what ought be observed. I therefore suggest—why, will become clear in the chapters on schizophrenia and psychopathy—that in many cases we must assign to cognition and its vicissitudes the central role in pathogenesis. The chapters on schizophrenia and psychopathy are expository; they suggest new, cognitive solutions to old puzzles.

Clinicians have very strong, positive sentiments about dreams. This lively interest is explainable perhaps by the distinguished service, so to speak, which dreams render to psychotherapy. However, dreams have something more to offer. Freud considered them most suitable for revealing the dynamic and structural characteristics of behavior.

Freud was not the pioneer of dream research, and many of his well-known theses were advanced by his predecessors. Griesinger (1845) was the first to propose that ". . . ideas in dreams and in psychoses have in common the characteristic of being *fulfillment of wishes*" (Freud, 1900). Scherner (1861) also explored symbols as the language specific to dreams. Indeed, Freud (1900) wholeheartedly appreciated Scherner's work, and called it "the most original and far-reaching attempt to explain dreaming as a special activity of the mind, capable of free expansion only during the state of sleep." Robert (1886) preceded Freud with a theory on the contribution of "day-residues" to dreams. Robert was of the opinion that "the reason why it is usually impossible to explain dreams is precisely because they are caused by sensory impressions of the preceding day which failed to attract enough of the dreamer's attention." Fechner (1889) suggested, though in different words, the idea of primary and secondary process: "In the course of a short discussion on the topic of dreams, the great Fechner puts forward the idea that *the scene of action of dreams is different from that of waking ideational life.* This is the only hypothesis that makes the special peculiarities of dream-life intelligible. . . . what is presented to us in these words is the idea of psychical locality." (Freud, 1900).

However, Freud was the first to propose the dream as the model phenomenon for a theory of psychology. Following this proposal of Freud, I will attempt here to elaborate the contribution of a cognitive approach (as opposed to drive-dynamics) to an understanding of dreams, and, by implication, of behavior in general.

Chapter Two

Psychopathology— A Cognitive View

Mental Health

PSYCHOPATHOLOGY IS, PERHAPS, the branch of psychology most influenced by Darwinian views and especially by the concept of adaptation. Adaptation is indeed an important process; it implies an interaction with environment, and it reminds us that "being" means "co-existing." However, the definition of *adaptation* usually emphasizes another aspect, namely, survival. Adaptation became the synonym for survival, and survival became the masterkey to an understanding of the phenomena of living. Color, form, structure, and behavior are regarded as subserving the leading function, adaptation—that is, survival. We are so used to this idea that we do not even feel obliged to prove it. Thus it may come as a surprise that the dominance of the concept of adaptation has been seriously challenged.

Portmann (1966) offers a host of morphological phenomena which are not wholly accounted for by invoking adaptation. The rather colorful aspects of sea-eagles or sea-anemones, for example, are neither helpful disguises nor instrumental in the mating of the sexes: they have no apparent functional value. Indeed, they are called "functionless" features. The point is, we meet such "functionless" features everywhere. The various patterns of leaves have no functional value, and they do not contribute to the struggle for survival; nor do the flowers need their characteristic charm to guarantee their pollination. Once one pays attention to these "functionless" phenomena, one must agree that adaptation, the process which fits an organism to survival in its environment, has no relevance to them. Portmann suggests separating the group of these gestalt-phenomena from the functions which make for survival, and calling them *self-actualizating.*

The label may sound peculiarly anthropomorphic. But we may assume that Portmann was fully aware of this danger. He was also aware that the living gestalten do more than just contribute to the survival of individual and species. The aesthetic achievements apparent in these gestalten, so it seems to Portmann, are as essential to an understanding of nature and life as are the numerous evidences of *the* function, survival. Nature, life, or whatever term one prefers is not reducible to mere existence. This is why the science of behavior, too, must acknowledge this wider scope, and must regard adaptation and self-actualization as complementary processes.

In fact, the difference between adaptation and self-actualization is one idea which has recurred in various formulations since time immemorial. In *Hamlet,* Polonious says, "This above all: to thine own self be true," which implies this difference, since the striving for genuineness and integrity may lead one to confront and oppose the environment, and may even jeopardize survival. Significantly, fitness to environment has never been regarded as the measure of integrity; nor has mere adaptation to circumstances been considered *per se* to be worthy of pursuit.

Both adaptation and self-actualization are usually accompanied by a sense of autonomy. Perhaps this feeling of self-determination is to a great extent illusory. No creature is wholly free, since everyone is born without choosing to be born, and dies without being able to change the direction of events. Despite these truths, we attribute to ourselves the ability to choose and decide. As Taylor (1960) sees it, life involves a continual series of choice points; it may be regarded as a kind of maze—a maze that continues throughout life. So important is the sense of autonomy that its obstruction can be no less fatal than the thwarting of adaptation or self-actualization.

Pondering the effects of extreme situations, Bettelheim (1960, 148) who was once a Nazi concentration-camp victim, observed: "By destroying man's ability to act on his own or to predict the outcome of his actions, they [the Nazis] destroyed the feeling that his actions had a purpose, so many prisoners stopped acting. But when they stopped acting they soon stopped living. What seemed to make the critical difference was whether or not the environment—extreme as it was—permitted (or promised) some minimal choices. . . ."

This then is our three-dimensional space: adaptation, self-actualization, and autonomy. Mental health is defined by an ability to adapt which is balanced by self-actualization and is accompanied by a sense of autonomy. The successful co-operation of these factors is essential for a meaningful, enjoyable life. And the failure of co-operation among the three factors leads to disturbed behavior.

The Nature of Behavior Disturbances

Behavior disturbances are many and varied. Is it possible to attribute to these diverse phenomena a common cause? Such a basic factor would be merely a frame, and every category of behavior disturbance would demand further, specific antecedents. Freud thought that there *is* such a common denominator in psychopathology: "The aetiology common to the onset of a psychoneurosis and of a psychosis always remains the same. It consists in a frustration, a non-fulfillment, one of those childhood wishes which are forever undefeated, and which are so deeply rooted in our phylogenetically determined organization" (1924, 151). The frustrated, erotic, and destructive impulses will regress to earlier phases of development and earlier attitudes toward objects, and at weak points where there are infantile fixations in the libidinal development, they will break through into consciousness and obtain discharge. In the final analysis all these phenomena are understood in terms of a mental energy and its vicissitudes. For Freud, then, the basis appropriate to psychology, normal and abnormal, is a theory like his theory of libido (1958, 447).

We assume, as the other natural sciences have taught us to expect, that in mental life some kind of energy is at work; but we have no data that enable us to come nearer to a knowledge of it by analogy with other forms of energy. We seem to recognize that nervous or psychical energy exists in two forms, one freely mobile and the other, by contrast, bound; we speak of cathexes and hypercathexes of the material of the mind and even venture to suppose that a hyper-cathexis brings about a sort of synthesis of

different processes—a synthesis in the course of which free
energy is transformed into bound energy. . . . we hold
firmly to the view that the distinction between the unconscious and the preconscious condition also lies in dynamic
relations of this same kind. . . .

The natural sciences referred to here concern the views
prevailing in nineteenth-century physics. The discovery
of the mechanical equivalent of heat, and the realization
that energy may be stored as potential energy and then
given out as work done by the body, led to the assumption
of a quantitative equivalence of cause and effect. Chains
of cause and effect were assumed, where every event was
the effect of a preceding one and the cause of a succeed-
ing one; and all these events were equal in energy. That
is to say, the relation between cause and effect was translated into the transfer of a determinable amount of energy from the first to the second. However, this view is
unacceptable for two reasons. First, there are release
mechanisms where a weak press on a button may cause
a shattering explosion; and second, there are summations
where an event of low energy (or of little importance)
may lead eventually to an effect disproportional to its own
loading. It is apparent that the law of conservation of
energy does not help us much in understanding behavior.
Nothing in instinctive activities, such as mating and
maternal behavior, suggests free or transferable energy.
They are simple variations in thresholds of activity, with
consequent differences in the value of the arousing stimulus. These are rather well-known considerations, and it is
certainly not by chance that Colby is not alone among
psychoanalytic writers in realizing the difficulties of a theory of behavior based upon the assumption of mental

energy and its vicissitudes. Unless energy can be measured in ergs, it is, as Ashby (1970) puts it, really a prestige-giving term for mere activity, busyness, or happening.

What is transferred is not energy, but rather signal. When we substitute signal—information—for energy, it becomes clear that the conflicts described by Freud imply a cognitive theory of behavior. Impulses by themselves do not evoke reflex-like defense mechanisms. Before any reaction is possible, the meaning of the impulses must be elaborated. Only after evaluating the impulse as compatible or incompatible with its internal or external standards can the organism accept or reject it. Indeed, Fenichel (1945) defined hysteric conversion as "not simple somatic expression of affects, but very specific representations of thoughts which can be retranslated from their 'somatic language' into the original word language."

A conversion symptom is the symbolic expression, by means of somatic malfunctions, of an emotionally charged idea. Therapeutic intervention may translate, or rather retranslate, the symbolically expressed idea into the original word language.

Alexander (1950) further elaborated this idea by stating that such symbolic expression is only known in the field of voluntary innervations. It seemed to him most improbable, however, that internal organs such as the liver or the small arterioles of the kidney can symbolically express ideas. "The vegetative organs are controlled by the autonomic nervous system, which is not in direct connection with ideational process."

Cognition emerges here as a central explanatory concept of behavior disturbances. The concept of psychosomatics may be pointed out as the most forceful catalyst in displaying the cognitive approach hidden in psychoanalysis, because, as we have seen, the justification of psychosomatics was a missing cognition.

In spite of this fact, many find it difficult, or even impossible, to accept cognition as the general frame of psychology, because it is inconsistent with the hierarchy of motives proposed by Freud. Freud (1915) thought that:

> . . . instinctual stimuli oblige the nervous system to renounce its ideal intention of warding off stimuli, for they maintain an incessant and unavoidable flux of stimulation, so we may probably conclude that instincts and not external stimuli are the true motive forces in the progress that has raised the nervous system with all its incomparable efficiency, to its present high level of development.

Although the evidence is inferential, the statement is unequivocal: most important among the possible motives of behaviour are instinctual stimuli. Add to this the concept of energy-transfer described above, and we have before us in a nutshell the psychodynamic (or rather, drive-dynamic) approach to an understanding of behaviour, normal as well as abnormal. The idea of dynamic equivalence between disparate phenomena due to an alleged transfer of displaced energy is, however, fallacious; we have seen that. I would like now to point out a few facts, unknown at the time Freud conceived his hierarchy of motives, which may help in establishing an outlook different from that of Freud—a cognitive view of psychopathology.

In an important experiment which did not receive the attention it deserves, Mészáros (1965), working with cats, electrically stimulated the splanchnic nerve (the most important of the visceral afferent nerves), and recorded the evoked potentials from the anterior ectosylvian gyrus.

Stimulation of the reticular substance for shorter periods, 100 to 200 msec., increased the evoked potentials. With increasing duration of stimulation, up to 5000 msec., the amplitude of the evoked potentials decreased, and the duration of the response became shorter. In contrast, the control sciatic (somatic) potentials were raised considerably with the increasing duration of reticular stimulation.

These results indicate that the reticular substance controls not only external inputs, but visceral impulses as well. Nevertheless, exteroceptive and proprioceptive impulses are facilitated by long-lasting reticular stimulation, while interoceptive ones are inhibited after an initial facilitation. In other words, while the reticular activating system lowers the threshold of the cerebral cortex to impulses of external origin, it strictly controls internal stimuli, and provisionally diminishes the sensitivity of the cortex to such impulses. That means, firstly, that instinctual stimuli are not able to maintain an incessant and inescapable flow of stimulation, as supposed by Freud. Rather, the propagation of stimuli underlying intero- as well as exteroception, is controlled by RAS. Secondly, the results of Mészáros's experiment are incompatible with the hypothesis that instincts and not external stimuli are the true motive force. In fact, the hierarchy of attention deployment revealed here causes one to suppose the opposite.

This change in the hierarchy of motives makes cognition the plausible candidate for a general model of psychopathology.

The Cognitive View

The central nervous system is fundamentally an information processing system; and it is questionable, to say the least, whether it is possible to propose a general theory of behavior without putting cognition in the center. Unconditional reflexes constitute the lowest level of the hierarchy of behavior. Some would even exclude them from the range of psychology. So it is highly significant that there is at least one unconditional reflex which, by definition, implies mental processes—that is, cognition. I mean the orienting reflex. The orienting reflex differs from other unconditioned reflexes in two respects. First, it is a nonspecific reaction to any change in the environment; second, repetition of the stimulus leads to its extinction (habituation), which does not happen with other unconditioned reflexes. These reactions to a change or novelty seem to imply comparison and judgment. Small wonder that Razran (1961) exclaimed, ". . . if any [innate behavior pattern] is accorded cognition status, the OR [orienting reflex] pattern is surely the most likely candidate. . . ."

Such is the situation regarding unconditional reflexes. Above this level no psychological phenomena can be explained without reference to cognition. Actually, we may restate this sentence, and say that psychology means those life phenomena which evidence cognition. We can trace the presence of cognition from the very beginning of life to its termination.

Hillman, in Bruner's laboratory, arranged feeding bottles which fed milk to babies every one or two seconds as long as they continued to suck for the whole of the interval. The one-day-olds adapted to the situation. But the point is that what they learned was not a stimulus-specific response, it was rather a *strategy*. Some of the babies reduced the rate of sucking impulses, and by extending the pauses between the impulses they created the required intervals (Bruner, 1970).

Clear evidence of reasoning in infants emerges very soon. The neonate maintains visual contact with a moving object by saccadic movements, but always focuses on that point where the moving object has just been seen. In contrast, the three-months-old infant *anticipates* the future position of the object by conjugate movements of the eyes (Wolf, 1967).

Infants seem also to be capable of conceptualizing. In one of his observations, Piaget (1936) put his face very close to that of his little daughter, Y., at 0: 11(4), and then alternately opened and closed his eyes. She watched him, laughed, and then while continuing to look at his eyes, slowly opened and closed her mouth. What happened here is only explainable by assuming conceptualization. "No concept of direct imitation, no concept of associated links could account for the fact that the child intuits from the father's behaviour the mode of *opening* and *closing*, regardless of the organ which is activated" (Wolf, 1967, 333).

We may be less reluctant to accept this conclusion if we take into consideration the similar performances of animals. The Gardners (1969) raised a young chimpanzee, Washoe, and taught her gestural language, the American Sign Language (ASL) used by the deaf. Both the Gardners and Washoe made history; and doubtless they will become as famous in comparative psychology as Kohler (1917) with his Sultan, and Premack (1971) with his Sarah. Through the ingenuity of the Gardners, Washoe was able to show behavioral evidence of conceptualization. For example, the chimpanzee first learned the sign for *open* with a particular door. This sign she then transferred to *open* for all closed doors, then to closed containers such as refrigerators, cupboards, drawers, briefcases, boxes, and jars. Washoe even spontaneously used it to request opening of the water faucet, and of a capped bottle of soda pop. Bronovski and Bellugi (1970) assert that the use of object-names Washoe had learned was not more narrow and context-bound than that of a human child.

Perhaps, one would prefer to speak here about transfer, as the Gardners did. But, since a concept is essentially a principle of classification, it follows that to transfer the sign *open* from the first referent to other members of this class of referents presupposes an act of classification, that is, a conceptualization. The Gardners report that when introducing new signs, they used specific referents for the initial training, and that Washoe herself extended the use of those signs far beyond the original training. The transfer, and the classification that was its basis were the contribution of Washoe. That is why we must speak here about conceptualization. If I understand rightly, Lashley (1942), too, ascribes to animals this feature of thinking. Analyzing the problem of stimulus equivalence, he stated that perceptual generalization may be traced by graduated steps, without change in fundamental principle, from the discriminative reactions of the rodent to the human insight which leads to important scientific generalizations. "This is the most elementary problem of cerebral function and I have come to doubt that any progress will be made toward a genuine understanding of nervous integration until the problem of . . . stimulus equivalence is solved."

Stimulus equivalence, generalization, transfer, all these terms converge in the question of similarity. Without generalization, that is, conceptualization, survival seems to be inconceivable. Since, as Heraclitus put it, we never step twice into the same river, the real value of learning lies in its help in mastering similar situations. How is similarity constituted? Is the perceiving of similarity a learned achievement or, is it an *a priori* category? Whatever the answer to this question, the point relevant to our discussion is that cognition is not an additional feature of behaviour; rather, it is at the very heart of being. Consequently, information processing, decision making, and their vicissitudes may be looked at as the general frame of psychopathology. Such a program will obviously not deny the existence of motives (after all, the drives to know and master are among them), but it will change the point of departure, the way of reasoning, and the definition of therapeutic aims and means.

The differences in outlook between drive dynamics and a cognitive approach are fairly well reflected in their respective emphases: the one on purposiveness and the other on systemic, structural, aspects of information processing. The dynamic point of view was summarized by Fenichel (1934) as follows:

> Freud ... favoured a conception which was to become the basis of psychoanalytic theory and which is known as the dynamic point of view. He maintained that given a special force within the ego which is engaged in defending the latter against the impact of certain experiences, it repels them, as it were; ... hence they are purposely diminuated from consciousness—they are *repressed*. Consequently ... hysterical amnesias are the result of a purposive (unconscious) desire to ignore. ...

The question crucial to this definition is whether the individual defends himself purposively (although unconsciously) against the conscious sensing of certain anxiety or pain-arousing experiences. Everywhere in psychology, whatever the field or level of function we are considering, individual differences are among the basic facts which cannot be disregarded. People are broadly alike, yet show great variations; they show countless versions of general plans. We may expect individual differences also in experiencing pain. But the question remains, what is it that these differences evidence: a deliberate decision of the system ego, or one of the structural properties of information processing?

Let us begin at the level of evoked potentials. Stimulation of a sensory receptor sets up a neural impulse that is forwarded along various pathways to the appropriate cortical area. If electrodes are placed on the scalp over this cortical area, the impulse can be picked up and recorded. This is the so-called evoked potential. It was found that the amplitude of an individual's average evoked responses (especially after 100 msec.) may increase, remain the same, or even decline with increasing stimulus (Buchsbaum, 1971). Since intensity is one of the factors of pain experience, the question arises of how to explain these differences in response to the same stimulus.

Evidence is available which favors the assumption that the differences in pain experience are regulated by the individual's information processing.

Using the kinesthetic aftereffect experiment, Petrie (1967) was able to show that a person's experience of the size of an object held between the fingers gradually changes; the reducer feels the object as smaller, while the augmenter feels the object has grown larger. The extent of this surprising concertina-like change in a few minutes is such that a eye glass case, for example, is experienced by the extreme reducer as half its original size, and by the extreme augmenter as half as large again.

In these experiments, the subject is blindfolded and

feels with the thumb and forefinger of the right hand the width of the measuring block. After that, with the thumb and forefinger of his other hand, he feels a long tapered bar and determines on the bar the place where it seems to be the same width as the measuring block. Then he rubs a wider stimulating block with his right thumb and forefinger. After 90 seconds of rubbing, he is again given the original measuring block and tapered bar, and compares them as before. The experienced width now will range from kinesthetic augmentation to reduction. This aftereffect is not modality-specific, maintains Petrie; what is being measured kinesthetically seems to be but one aspect of the general tendency for the reducer to diminish the perception of stimulation and for the augmenter to enlarge it.

What makes this experiment relevant to our discussion is Petrie's finding that these perceptual aftereffects co-vary with pain experiences. Augmenters tolerate bodily pain least well, while the reducers tolerate it best. The differences in reduction between those with less and those with greater tolerance for pain reached the 5 per cent level of confidence after only 90 seconds of kinesthetic stimulation. However, this statement calls for an important qualification. There are various categories of pain, and in some of them the augmenters will win the contest.

The sensory deprivation experiment shows how much the maintenance of our adaptive mental organization depends on the stream of continuous stimuli: being sensorily deprived or sensorily bombarded are the two extremes of this continuum. We may hypothesize that one of the two end-points will be experienced as "pain" by the reducer and the other one by the augmenter. Leveling the intensity of his input, the reducer in a sensory-deprivation situation may very soon experience the disorganization of his control; whereas the augmenter will be able to compensate for the scarcity of input by experiencing it more intensely. On the other hand, the augmenter may suffer earlier from an overload of stimuli. The absence of stimulation may be intolerable to a reducer, but not to an augmenter. Petrie examined volunteers for the sensory-deprivation experiment in an iron lung, and she found, as expected, that augmenters tolerate deprivation of stimuli longer than do reducers.

It is apparent that the reducer eagerly seeks contact, is physically active, and relies heavily on stimuli provided by extero- and proprioception for maintaining his identity and his orientation in reality. At the same time the consciously experienced stimuli are leveled off, their intensity is reduced or even not perceived. Is such stimulus-hunger a consequence of the meagerness of conscious experiences? Or is the reducing itself a defense against an agitating flux of stimuli? In other words, does the story begin with an extravert who reacts defensively by reducing? Or do we begin with the reducing, which is then counterbalanced by extravert behavior? Whatever the answer to this question, it is one of the vicissitudes of information processing. Both possibilities have nothing whatever to do with psychodynamics, although superficially it may seem so. Certainly, the kinesthetic figural aftereffects will not presuppose a struggle between drive and defence; nor would such a struggle explain the position that the subject occupies in the augmenter—moderate—reducer continuum in registering stimulus intensity. Subjective pain experiences, instead of being regulated by mechanisms of defences against instinctual impulses, appear here as particular cases of information processing.

I have studied a further aspect of pain experience, that of susceptibility to distraction. The subjects were amputees who had phantom limb pain, and those who had a phantom limb without pain. Most amputees report feeling a phantom limb almost immediately after amputation of an arm or leg. The phantom limb is usually described as having a tingling feeling and a definite shape that resembles the real limb before amputation. Some of the amputees report pain in the phantom limb. It may be occasional or continuous, and is described as cramping, shooting, burning, or crushing. A common complaint is that the phantom hand is clenched, fingers bent over the thumb and digging into the palm, so that the whole hand is tired and painful.

It was hypothesized that the amputee who feels a painless phantom limb is interference-prone and cannot withstand distracting stimuli; while the amputee with a painful phantom limb is able to shut out the interfering stimuli of a configuration, and to maintain focused attention. This disposition to concentrate tends to reduce the redundancy of input channels and at the same time creates a high redundancy of information sampling from the limited field to which the amputee is giving his attention. The result will be an increased brightness and salience of the object of perception (Silverman, 1968)—in this case, of the pain.

Since the selectiveness factor of attention was pointed out as one of the preconditions of phantom limb pain, subjects were given Jackson's Embedded Figures Test (EFT). The subject's task here was to locate a simple geometric figure embedded in a more complex figure. Those who perform well on the EFT are less distracted by irrelevant stimuli, and are able to sustain a distinct focus of attention.

The results showed a convincing difference (at the .005, one-tailed, significance level) between the performances of the two groups. Subjects with phantom limb pain perform better on the Embedded Figures Test than subjects with no phantom limb pain. That is to say, those subjects with the attentional disposition to shut out interfering stimuli and concentrate upon a small segment, thereby enhancing its perceived magnitude and salience, possess the necessary basis for sensitivity to pain. Hence exaggerated pain experience, and its opposite under the same conditions, may be understood as an outcome of a characteristic form of information processing.

The same subjects with painful phantom limbs who perform well on the Embedded Figures Test were also found to habitually recall their dreams. On the other hand, subjects with painless phantom limbs are habitual nonrecallers. The differential frequencies of dream recall by the two types vary at the .025, one-tailed, significance level. These differences in habitual dream recall may be interpreted as a further consequence of the selectiveness factor of attention. People who can resume waking awareness and still focus on the dream will remember their dream. People who are more stimulus and situation-bound will find it difficult to carry over their dream to awareness by singling it out from the impressions of the awakening process; they are habitual nonrecallers of dreams.

We may push the matter one step further. Petrie (1967), in one of her experiments, was able to show that the higher the extraversion score one had, as measured by the Maudsley Personality Inventory, the better he tolerated bodily pain. And conversely, those who tolerated the stress of sensory deprivation best have the lowest extraversion score. There seems to be a certain overlapping between the concept of extraversion-reducing and the concept of introversion-augmenting. In view of this possibility, certain facts in regard to the so-called "masking effect" may appear in a new perspective.

If a disc is presented to a subject for a period of 15 milliseconds and upwards, it can be seen clearly. If an annulus is presented some time after the disc has been withdrawn (at about 86 milliseconds), then the annulus may wipe out the percept of the disc. The disc is "masked." As the establishing of a percept is also a function of the time at the disposal of the nervous system, this masking effect may reflect the duration of cortical arousal necessary to processing. Now, accepting the assumption that cortical arousal is, in fact, an outcome of the dynamism between arousal and inhibition, Eysenck hypothesizes individual differences in the critical period during which the masking effect may occur. Extraverts are charracterized by a high basal cortical arousal, and are prone to cortical inhibition; under the specified time conditions they may not succeed in separating and registering the two percepts. Introverts have a higher threshold of inhibition, therefore they will have the time necessary for stabilizing two separate percepts. Indeed, McLaughlin and Eysenck (1967) reported a correlation of 0.36 between extinction period and extraversion. The critical period for the masking effect is shorter in extraverts; they are more susceptible to "forgetting" as a result of the masking effect.

In sum, we may say that extraverts reduce the intensity of stimuli, neutral as well as emotionally meaningful; they

are habitual nonrecallers of dreams; and they are susceptible to a pronounced (i.e., early) masking effect. Now the
nonrecalling of dreams, reduced pain experience, and
many of the masking effects are pointed out as typifying
the influence of repression. In point of fact, however, they
result from a rather complex and individually characteristic way of information processing.

That is not to say that motivated forgetting does not
exist. It does exist, certainly. But I have the feeling that we
have grossly exaggerated the rate of occurrence of those
"purposive, though unconscious" repulsions of experiences from consciousness. The case of habitual nonrecalling of dreams shows it. Recalling of dreams is determined,
first of all, by an ability to segmentalize the field of attention; or, on the contrary, by a susceptibility to interference of distracting stimuli. It must be strongly emphasized that the motivation to forget may take advantage,
secondarily, of the existing structure of information processing.

Also, we have taken too lightly the fact that many people do not take refuge in repression. They are not able to
repress, as we are accustomed to say. Some of these people, however, not only do not ignore a painful experience,
they actually augment its intensity. These facts remind us
that pain, anxiety, dreams, and so on, are informations
perceived and elaborated in an individually characteristic
way. We must begin our attempt at understanding by
describing the ways and modes of information processing.

This is not the first time that such a approach has been
formulated. Gardner *et al.* (1959) suggested a system of
cognitive control principles. However, while acknowledging the necessity of a cognitive reorientation, those
researchers were reluctant to draw the final conclusion

from their own work, namely, that we must abandon drive dynamics and adopt a cognitive approach.

The cognitive controls proposed by Gardner and others involve levelling-sharpening, equivalence range (preference for broad or narrow conceptual categories), scanning, tolerance for unrealistic experiences, and field-articulation. Attention was given mostly to the cognitive control of levelling-sharpening. The Schematizing Test was the criterion used to select levellers and sharpeners. The subjects were asked to judge the sizes of 150 squares individually projected onto a screen. After the initial presentation, the smallest square was dropped and replaced with a slightly larger one. The size of the squares gradually increased. Some subjects kept track of the general trend of increase in size, and also maintained accurate ranking of the individual squares; while others tended to blur distinctions among the squares and lagged behind the trend of increase. The latter are "levellers."

Levelling-sharpening of perceptual stimuli indicates a mode of organization similar to other cognitive functions. The associations of levellers are organized in a rather global and undifferentiated way. They remain focused around one dominant idea, the assimilative force of which limits the occurence of new and different themes. Regarding the organization of recall, Holzman and Gardner (1960) found that the anxiety-arousing motive of a popular story (the killing of children as "retribution" in *The Pied Piper*) was retained by only 26 per cent of the leveller narrators, as against 58 per cent of the sharpener narrators. The number of correctly remembered elements in the story differed as well: 3.3 for levellers, 5.6 for sharpeners. Levelling-sharpening also controls the impact of drives on behaviour. Holzman and Gardner (1959) have shown that extreme repressers are also extreme levellers. However, the converse is not true: not all levellers rely upon repression as their principal defence. Among the subjects with lower reliance upon repression (as measured by Rorschach Test) are sharpeners as well as levellers.

This is one of the important attempts to defend psychoanalysis by liberalizing the mechanisms of defence. In the opinion of these investigators, extreme levelling reflects a basic characteristic of memory organization. It might be regarded as a necessary but insufficient condition for the emergence of repression as a major defence. Formulating it in a language Gardner and the others did not use, but with which they could agree, we may say that levelling-sharpening is one of the modes of information processing pertinent mainly to the formation of memory schemata. This cognitive function is the basis; repression is its possible outgrowth, provided, of course, that additional conditions exist.

The cognitive orientation is further underlined by Holzman and Gardner's suggestion that anticipation may be another process parameter essential to an understanding of the levelling-sharpening principle. Subjects who lag behind the trend of increasing size of squares in the Schematizing Test may be influenced by an anticipation of smallness built up early in the test. In other situations, such as time-error tests, their slowness in changing anticipations may show itself in exaggerated experiences of contrast. The distance between the actual experience and its anticipation causes a pronounced contrast effect, and therefore the size or weight of the new stimulus will be underestimated. This underestimation of the subsequent stimulus should be labeled as levelling.

We are now on our way to having the outlines of a cognitive psychopathology. But no—Gardner *et al.* suddenly change their course and suggest that a sharpener may have available large quantities of free energy for hypercathexis of new stimuli, which renders them unusually clear and distinct. Levellers on the other hand, may show large assimilation effects because they have limited amounts of energy for hypercathexis of new stimuli. "Thus, extremely repressive persons could be levellers because the massive countercathexis of ideas held out of consciousness uses up large quantities of energy that would otherwise be available for hypercathexis of new stimuli" (138).

By now it is not clear what is explained by what—levelling by repression, or repression by levelling. If levelling and sharpening are explained by personality differences in the availability of free energy to hypercathect, then the idea of countercathexis would lead us to expect a linear relationship, such that the heavier the repression, the less free energy and the more the memory organization will function by levelling—that is, by assimilating new information to the old. But contrary to this expectation, Holzman and Gardner found that sharpeners as well as levellers may rely on repression, though not extremely. Where then do these sharpeners obtain the free energy for hypercathexis, and why do their fellow levellers not have it?

This dilemma can be solved by abandoning speculations concerning psychic energy and by accepting a cognitive approach. Information is processed in order to make decisions. These processes, the systems subserving them, and their behavioral consequences define our perspective.

Experimental neuroses

These conclusions may be clarified by a short discussion of the experimental neuroses of animals. Massermann (1961) trained his animals (rats, cats, dogs, or monkeys) to respond to the flash of a light or the sound of a bell by opening a box to secure a pellet of food. These animals were then further trained to press a switch to operate these feeding signals at will. When the feeding signals were stopped by disconnecting the switch or locking the food box, the animals continued to strike the disc switch vigorously and also showed signs of a behavioral arousal. Soon, however, the animals adapted to the new situation by ignoring the signals and the food box. If however, on several irregularly spaced occasions, at the moment of reaching the food the animals were subjected to a mild but unexpected air blast or electric shock, they developed an experimental neurosis.

Some refused to eat in or out of the experimental cage, and actually starved themselves into a state of morbid inanition. Others would eat only food pellets of a shape or composition other than those used in the experiment. They also showed motor dysfunctions, ranging from cataleptic immobility to continuous hyperactivity. Between these extremes lay compulsion-like behaviors: a hungry animal might turn on its back at a feeding signal and claw at the light in a peculiarly stereotyped manner. One neurotic dog developed the elaborate ritual of circling the food box three times and then bowing on its forepaws before attempting to feed. In addition, many animals, despite adequate artificial feeding, showed disturbances of gastrointestinal function such as diarrhea or constipation, with a persistent loss of weight. Sexual behavior, too, changed. There was complete loss, or conversely, indiscriminate intensification, of sexual activity. Neurotic monkeys became homosexual or autoerotic. One female vervet continuously manipulated her axillae, anus, and genitalia, and her male companion almost flayed his penis by nearly unremitting auto-fellatio over a period of weeks. Some monkeys appeared to have hallucinations: while they refused food available in their food boxes, they were observed trying to pick nonexistent pellets from various surfaces of the cage or from out of the air, and chewing and swallowing these imaginary tidbits with apparent relish.

Comparing these dramatic changes in behavior with their antecedents, one cannot help but but be puzzled. Are those unexpected air-blasts truly such traumatic experiences? And if so, how explain their effects, which seem to pervade all the major realms of life? Fear in the sense of dread of injury need not be involved at all, Masserman (1966) asserts. Equally serious and lasting neurotigenic effects can be induced by facing the animal with difficult choices among mutually exclusive satisfactions, such as food versus mothering, or exploration versus sex.

The conflict emphasized by Masserman is the same insoluble problem we have met in the Pavlovian experimental neurosis. There, a dog was presented with a circle which was followed by food, and by an ellipse which was not. Having taught the dog this discrimination, the experimenter begins to round the ellipse and to flatten the circle. Since a patterned order of presentation might help the dog to learn adaptively, he presents the changing figures randomly. Finally, these two objects become indistinguishable to the animal, and at this point the dog begins to show severe disturbances. What has happened here?

Nothing more than this: ". . . the experimenter succeeds

in communicating to the dog a message about the contingency patterns in which it is to find itself, and this message happens to be an untrue message. The dog is in a probabilistic situation, but the experimenter has convinced the dog that it is in a discrimination situation" (Bateson, 1963). This message was underlined during the period when discrimination was difficult, but still possible. If, however, the same experiment is started with a naive dog and the preliminary training in discrimination is omitted, "the dog does not go crazy ... it will gamble on the difference."

A blurring of their cognitive map—which is what Bateson's analysis means—paralyzes these animals by disturbing their ability to cope with the situation. The resulting extremely high arousal ends up in behavior stereotypes, psychosomatic reactions, sexual aberrations, a change in social heirarchy, and even hallucinations. The point, then, is cognition.

Chapter Three

Have Symptons A
Hidden Meaning?

VIEWING COGNITION as the general frame of behaviour, normal and abnormal, we have now to point out the consequences of this approach to an understanding of the various phenomena of psychopathology.

Following the conventional classification of neuroses, psychopathy, and psychoses, we will turn first to the neuroses. Freud (1926, 103) suggested a definition of neurotic symptoms, which may serve as a point of departure for our discussion.

> We cannot therefore describe the fear belonging to this phobia as a symptom. If "Little Hans," being in love with his mother, had shown fear of his father, we should have no right to say that he had a neurosis or a phobia. His emotional reaction would have been entirely comprehensible. What made it a neurosis was one thing alone: the replacement of his father by a horse. It is this displacement, then, which has a claim to be a symptom . . .

This definition contains two assumptions: 1) A perpetuated unconscious inner psychic conflict ends up in a malfunction. 2) This malfunction substitutes itself by symbolic equations for the original conflict. Discovering the original conflict reveals the hidden meaning of the malfunction. The essence is the unconscious conflict; the malfunction, the symptom, only indicates it.

The definition of psychosomatics proposed by Alexander (1950) was a logical derivative of Freud's view. Alexander thought that symbolic expression is only known in the field of voluntary innervations. Both hysterical symptoms and vegetative neuroses are sequelae of psychological stress; they are basically different, however, in their psychodynamics and neurophysiology. Elevation of blood pressure, for example, under the influence of rage is a physiological component of the total phenomenon of rage. It is the concomitant rather than the symbolic expression of it; high blood pressure is not an hysterical symptom, but a psychosomatic disorder.

This differentiation was also supported by the then-prevailing theories of learning. The cerebrospinal skeletal muscle responses operate on the external environment, while the activities controlled by the autonomic system maintain the internal environment. A corollary of this dichotomy was the assumption that the organism's behaviour consists of two basic categories, differing in the learning processes by which they can be modified. Accordingly, many psychologists distinguished between two types of learning: classical or respondent conditioning, and instrumental or operant learning. The classically conditionable responses are involuntary responses of the autonomic nervous system, while the instrumentally-learned behaviours are voluntary responses of the central nervous system. This dichotomy was considerably strengthened by the apparent impossibility of conditioning GSR and vasoconstriction by instrumental methods.

However, the scene has changed since then. During the last few years a slowly growing literature has shown the possibility of gaining voluntary control over autonomic functions, such as brain waves, heart beat, and blood pressure (Kamiya, 1968). The important point here is that this exciting expansion of voluntary control is achieved by cognition; by supplying information to subjects, visually or otherwise, to the effect that their brain waves were now within range of 8 to 12 per second, that their hearts were beating slowly, or that their blood pressure was high. Supplied with no more than this, the subjects were able to prolong the occurrence of the alpha brain wave, to change their heart beat, or to maintain a low level of blood pressure. For example, Lang (1970) demonstrated that we are able, under certain limits, to "drive" our heartbeat. In his experiment, the subject watched a small spot of light on a screen in front of him. Whenever the interval between two heartbeats was exactly one second, the light appeared on a vertical line in the center of the screen. When the interval was longer or shorter, the light moved off to the right or left. The subject was told to keep the light within a narrow road often less than 90 milliseconds wide—from 9.55 to 1.045 milliseconds. He soon became quite skilled at keeping the light on the road, and his ability improved with practice.

In a clinical setting, Weiss and Engel (1971) have shown that patients with premature ventricular contractions (PVCs) are able to control this arrhythmia. Here, three differently colored lights at the foot of the bed provided the patient with information about his cardiac function: high, low, and correct heart rate. Gradually, the patient became aware of PVCs through his own sensations and

without the help of the lights. The results showed clear
evidence of PVC control by patients, and maintenance of
control while at home.

Or, to take another example, Basmajian (1972) was able
to demonstrate voluntary control over skeletal muscles.
The nerve cell body, its axon, terminal branches, and all
the muscle fibers supplied by these branches constitute a
motor unit. Subjects undergoing motor unit training are
given auditory and visual displays of their individual
myoelectric potentials, recorded by means of intramuscu-
lar electrodes. The cues provide the subjects with an
awareness of the twitching of individual motor units.
They learn in a few minutes to control this activity, and
can give any required response with only the feedback
information as a guide. Some persons can be trained to
gain control of isolated motor units to such a degree that,
with both visceral and aural cues shut off, they can establish the selected unit fixing without any conscious awareness other than the assurance—after the fact—that they
have succeeded.

These examples on voluntary control of the autonomic
nervous system make obsolete the traditional dichotomy
of voluntary responses controlled by the central nervous
system and involuntary responses controlled by the autonomic nervous system. This dichotomy, as Lang puts it, is
now out the window; neuroanatomical and neurophysiological evidence against such a distinction has been ac-
cumulating for some time. It is now a well-established
view that visceral functions are represented at the highest
level of the brain, the cerebral cortex. Therefore, the
differentiation between hysteria and psychosomatic disorder, as proposed by Alexander, has lost its ground. He
thought that "the vegetative organs are controlled by the

autonomic nervous system, which is not in direct connection with ideational processes." If, however, voluntary as well as autonomic systems are cognitively controlled, there is no reason for not assigning to every malfunction the possibility that it symbolically expresses thoughts and emotions. We have to give up the categories of psychosomatics, vegetative neuroses, organ neuroses; all these concepts now appear unfounded. We have only one major category of behaviour disturbances, psychoneuroses, the realm of which is defined, according to Freud, by a displaced—that is symbolized—expression of an unconscious conflict.

The terms *displacement* and *symbolic expression* are used here as synonyms, but in fact each of them has a different aura. Symbolization implies a message; the sufferer expresses something important in a nonconventional manner. Szasz (1961) is foremost among those who view this approach as the correct interpretation of neurotic symptoms. An understanding of suicide as a cry for help is another example of psychopathology as a symbolized communication. Displacement, on the other hand, hints at an inner psychic conflict. "A symptom is a sign and a substitute for an instinctual satisfaction which has remained in abeyance: it is a consequence of the process of repression" (Freud, 1926, 91). Here a struggle between drive and defence is pointed out; this ambiguity has never been resolved in psychoanalytic literature.

Displacement is related to the concept of mental energy, libido. The libido, dammed up by a repression, obtains discharge by regressing to earlier phases of development and earlier attitudes toward objects; while symbolization, as a construct of communication, conveys meaning and is indifferent to questions of energetics.

Also, communication stresses the relation of the individual to his environment, while displacement hints at an event belonging to the deepest inner self. And, finally, psychopathology as a communication would not necessitate the assumption of conflicting psychic systems, id and ego; whereas displacement certainly does. In an often quoted paper, Schur (1955) states that "Vomiting in infancy frequently is an early expression of rejection of the mother and therefore symbolic in meaning." It is not clear what he meant by assigning symbolic meaning to vomiting, nor how the infant could directly express a rejection of the mother. At any rate, this symbolization was certainly not thought to be caused by an inner psychic conflict. Unlike symbolization, displacement, as already pointed out, is the effect of repression.

Thus, symbolizations and displacement are actually not ambiguous synonyms, but rather incompatible concepts. Freud's theory of neurotic symptoms is, in fact, a theory of displacement of cathexes and not a theory of communication. True, he dealt with symbols, as in dreams, but not with symbolization as a way of conveying information to another. According to Freud, then, the meaning of a neurotic symptom is unravelled by retranslating it from its displaced appearance to the original, now unconscious conflict. The malfunction is only symptomatic of the hidden, pathogenic event; the real problem is covered. That real problem, what is it?

Homosexuality—real or metaphorical?

Freud thought that the paranoid patient's complaints of being persecuted are not to be taken at face value. In fact, these patients are troubled by something else. The really operative factor lies in the homosexual components of their affective life. "The development of delusions never fails to unmask these relations and to trace back the social feelings to their roots in a purely sensual erotic wish" (1911, 445). This he demonstrated by an analysis of the autobiography of his patient, Schreber.

This patient was hospitalized in a condition of acute psychosis. He had complained that he lived for a long time without a stomach, without intestines, and without many other organs. He also thought from time to time that he swallowed part of his own larynx with his food. He believed that he was dead and decomposing, but also that his body was being handled in all kinds of revolting ways. He was so much occupied with these pathological phenomena that he would sit rigid and motionless for hours. During this acute period, he tried many times to commit suicide. Slowly, as the storm period subsided, it became apparent that the patient had evolved a delusional system. He asserted that he had a mission to redeem the world and to restore mankind to its lost state of bliss. In order to fulfill this mission of redemption, he had to be transformed into a woman.

In the opinion of Freud, this patient's primary delusion was that of emasculation, which at the beginning was conceived as persecution and a threat of sexual abuse. This delusion was related to his role as Redeemer in only a secondary way; and Freud points out that it merely requires a slight correction of Schreber's mode of expression to enable us to divine the fact that the patient was in fear of sexual abuse at the hands of his physician. At the base of this fear was a homosexual wish to love a person of the same sex and an inner struggle against this impulse.

All the principal forms of the paranoid mechanism can

be represented as contradictions of the single proposition: "I (a man) love him (a man)." The proposition: "I (a man) love him" actually loudly asserts its opposite. As Freud put it—"I do not love him—I hate him." The proposition "I hate him" then becomes transformed by projection into another one: "He hates (persecutes) me." The delusion thus is only a symptom that indicates the real problem: an inner psychic struggle against a homosexual impulse.

Ovesey (1955) published a case very similar to that of Schreber's. The patient, 34 years old, married, with two children, was suffering from incipient paranoid schizophrenia. His principal symptom was his conviction that he was changing into a woman. Alarmed by this danger, he went to an endocrinologist and asked for injections of male hormones in the hope that they would halt the imagined transformation. According to the patient, his voice was higher, his hips were larger, and he was beginning to walk with a flounce. He repeatedly examined his genitals for signs of shrinkage. He misinterpreted the remarks and actions of people around him, believing that they referred to him as effeminate and as a homosexual. These ideas of reference, "almost imperceptibly but quite definitely" were beginning to shade off into delusions of persecution. The patient also confessed to repetitive fantasies in which he performed fellatio on his uncle, a man whom the patient greatly admired.

This case seems to support Freud's view. A homosexual wish fantasy and the perceiving of it as a deadly danger are at the core of this patient's illness. In Ovesey's opinion, however, what his patient really suffered from was a success phobia. He was unable to enjoy success and achievement of ambitious goals because of the fear of retaliation from his competitors; this problem was metaphorically expressed by pseudo-homosexuality. The patient was born into a family of giants; he himself was only five feet six. His whole life was arranged around an endless competitive effort to disprove his own convictions of inferiority. Indeed, he succeeded in advancing with phenomenal rapidity to a top position of a large organization. Significantly, the intensification of his anxiety coincided with his promotion. Precisely the same happened also to Freud's patient, Schreber. He suffered twice from a nervous breakdown: the first time while he was a candidate for election to the Reichstag, and again, when he entered upon his new duties as president of the Supreme Court. Schreber, a judge by profession, was notified of his promotion to the president of the Senate in June. He took up his duties on the first of October, and his illness set in at the end of that month.

Ovesey's patient abruptly resigned from his job. He decided to retire to a small country town to live out his days free from competitive strain by running a gasoline station. The peak of his vocational success was his moment of greatest danger, and it initiated a delusional materialization of the expected retaliation. Therefore, in this and similar cases, we have to differentiate between pseudo-homosexuality and the real core of the illness which lies elsewhere, in the need for dependency. As Ovesey says (168), "The desire for dependency through the paternal love of a father-substitute is the most superficial form of the dependency fantasy. The same fantasy on a deeper unconscious level is integrated in a more primitive fashion through the equation, breast-penis. The patient who resorts to this equation attempts to gratify his dependency needs through the oral or anal incorporation of the stronger man's penis."

Here we are. We have to decide between the theory of "an outburst of homosexual libido" and a "success phobia" with pseudo-homosexual features. The question is, which is real and which is metaphorical? It is hardly imaginable that we can succeed in solving such a riddle. The moment that we regard phenomena as merely transfigurations of the essence, the "real" reality, there are no limits on symbolization. We are making the assumption then that we will understand life better by disregarding phenomenology. If we decide that sexual strivings are more important than the need for dependency, dependency will be interpreted as an indication of the "real" motive, sexuality. This is what Freud has done. If, on the other hand, we decide that dependency is the "real" need, we will regard its frustration as expressed in a pseudosexual symbolic language. This is Ovesey's opinion.

Actually, there are a few more possibilities available. Rank (1936) suggests that will is the true motive of behavior. "One might say that this is sexuality, as Freud originally assumed, provided one understands it not only in a broader but in the broadest sense of the word. . . . This generic sexual compulsion which, as sexual attraction, is the root of the Freudian Oedipus complex, when it is actually completely aroused . . . is so strong and dominates the individual so extremely that soon he begins to defend himself against its domination, just because it is domination, something that interferes dictationally with his own will as individual" (281). The individual defends himself against the sexual drive because it would force him under the rule of a strange will, just at the time when his ego has only begun to breathe a little freely, released from the pressure of other peoples' authoritative wills. The individual would like to maintain his slowly won autonomy without subjecting himself to an alien, sexual will.

It may happen that an individual cannot accept his own will, and cannot admit it or affirm it, but is compelled to reject and deny it. This denial causes, secondarily, guilt and inferiority feelings. "Herein lies . . . the origin of the sexual guilt feeling, since the guilt for willing falls into the sexual sphere by displacement . . ." (283). Who has seen the truth, Freud, Rank, or Ovesey?

Kohut (1971) states that the psychoanalytic approach means using the name of the most conspicuous or clearly delimited manifestation of a group or series of developmentally, generically, and dynamically related phenomena as a term for the whole class. This "has become a well-established practice . . . since Freud referred to all libidinal drive elements as sexual ones *a potiori* and by reason of their origin. . . . In other words, Freud used the term 'sexual' not only for genital sexuality but also for the pregenital drive elements . . . because genital sexuality was the more important (and thus the better known) of these two related groups of phenomena" (25).

The weak point of this reasoning is that of relatedness. How can we prove that phenomenologically different behaviours are dynamically related? The method of proof, as is well known, is free association. But free associations are not free at all. The expectations of the therapist and the wish of the patient to please him have a decided influence. Psychoanalysts hear about topics reported in a language they are used to; but so do analytical psychologists. Under such conditions, matters that emerge as dynamically related must be regarded as artifacts of the situation, rather than the revelations of hidden facts. Patients tend, while free associating, "to bring up precisely the kind of phenomenological data which confirms the theories and interpretations of their analysts!" (Marmor, 1962).

The interpretations, remembrances, thoughts, and feelings evoked by free association do not explain themselves and even less do they explain their relatedness to each other; the therapist has to reveal the meanings made apparent by them, and interpret accordingly. Alas, by interpreting, we have come full circle, and have landed ourselves in the selfsame arbitrariness we thought to overcome by depending on free associations. The therapist determines whether the meaning of the patient's association is revealed. There are no objective criteria for judging the therapist's decisions. He may require association until a picture emerges which will fit his own, not unbiased understanding. Or, he may make his judgment first, and then deal with the material supplied to him rather loosely. As a matter of fact, Freud, Rank, and Ovesey arrived at their divergent conclusions by interpreting their patients' free associations. The decision as to whether sexuality or dependency or will is the "really" important motive does not follow from an analysis of behavior; rather, it precedes it. The road to the paradise of unlimited possibilities, where the truth has as many faces as the number of its seekers, is paved by interpretations.

Freud thought that interpretations as well as free associations take advantage of symbols. Symbols are part of our earliest heritage, dating from the period of our lives when language developed; but although we all use symbols, for example, in dreams, a patient "does not understand them unless an analyst interprets them to him, and even then he is reluctant to believe the translation. If he makes use of one of the many common figures of speech in which this symbolism is recorded, he is obliged to admit that its true sense has completely escaped him" (1939, 98).

Wherefrom does the analyst learn the true meaning of what all others are unable to grasp? Or does he indeed know? The attempt to arrive at the "true" but hidden meaning of a phenomenon by means of free association and interpretation of symbols resembles the pursuit of *fata morgana.*

But if this is true, then displacement, the very heart of Freud's theory of neuroses, is called into question. In his view, what made Little Hans's phobia a neurosis "was one thing alone: the replacement of his father by a horse. It is this displacement . . . which has a claim to be a symptom." This definition of a neurotic symptom requires a differentiation between the real conflict and its displaced expression. But precisely this differentiation, that is, the identification of the basic motive, is made difficult, or, rather, impossible by the biases and preconceived ideas inherent in the concept of dynamic relatedness.

Repression

A similar difficulty of testability besets the concept that is the twin of displacement, namely, repression. This concept was summarized by Fenichel (1934) as follows:

> Freud . . . maintained that a special force within the ego is engaged in defending the latter against the impact of certain experiences, it repels them, as it were . . . hence they are purposely eliminated from consciousness—they are *repressed.* Consequently . . . hysterical amnesias are the result of a purposive (unconscious) desire to ignore.

Since nonretrievability for recall may be caused by motivational as well as nonmotivational factors like fatigue, distraction, and so on, it is important to establish criteria to reliably distinguish between them. The criterion proposed by Freud is of distortion. "The mechanism of repression becomes accessible to us only by our deducing that mechanism from the *outcome* of the repression" (1915, 154). Viewing the distortions imposed on a thought while it passes from the first to the second psychical system, we infer the process of repression. "We can lay down no general rule as to what degree of distortion and remoteness is necessary before the resistance on the part of the conscious is removed" (150). The degree of distortion differs from individual to individual, but it will be inevitable in every case. But Freud's very definition of repression makes it impossible to test whether some mental content ever reappears as it was before repression. Consequently, it is impossible to prove the existence of repression.

If, for example, a dream reproduces photographically, as it were, some forgotten experience, then by definition this experience did not emerge from the first psychical system, and therefore does not prove the participation of id wishes in dreams. If, however, dream images or stories distort some real though forgotten impression, we can never substantiate the argument for repression, because this substantiation presupposes a comparison between the original wish and its distorted and displaced reappearance. But repressed thoughts by becoming conscious will always be distorted, so how can we know their original meaning? How can we prove that their actual presentation is remote from the earlier experience and is disguised relative to it?

This puzzle is especially striking as far as symbols are concerned. Freud thought that the true sense of symbols escapes us unless we are informed about it by an analyst.

By what method did he discover it, though, and how did he validate his discovery? ". . . the archaic heritage . . . can . . . become active—that is [it] can advance to consciousness from its unconscious state in the id, even though in an altered and distorted shape" (1938, 101). But that is precisely why we ask how and by what means the analyst is able to define the "true" sense of a symbol if it is impossible for an idea to pass from the first to the second psychical system without alterations. The definition of repression attributes to unconscious mental contents the character of being never really perceivable, very much like Kant's *Ding an sich*. But then, if it never will reveal its real face, we will never be able to understand its true sense. Both repressed impressions and phylogenetic memories can never appear in their original or true form in consciousness, due to repression and the inevitable distortion that occurs when repression is lifted; therefore, one cannot invoke the concept of repression while explaining at the same time the *real* meaning of the repressed content. Freud's view that the unconscious ". . . has no access to conscious except *via the preconscious* in passing through which its excitatory process is obliged to submit to modifications" (1900, 540) is a nontestable statement.

Is it possible to have a theory of behavior without the concept of repression? We have become so accustomed to the idea of repression that it may seem hardly imaginable to us. Yet, this is the position we are led to by the impasse created by the definition of repression. Actually, this is not the first time that repression has been viewed skeptically. Fairbairn (1954) once wrote: "I must record the opinion that the eclipse of the concept of dissociation, which has accompanied the explanatory ascendancy of the concept of repression, has not been altogether an unmixed gain."

Also Luborsky (1967) urges a restriction of the use of repression. Recalling the Freud-Breuer disagreement about "hypnoid states," he observes (204) that "Freud at that time stressed defense as the reason for the construction of excluded ideational complexes. Breuer thought hypnoid states were the 'cause and necessary condition' of many hysterias . . . but obviously they play a contributory role." Luborsky's attempts to reinstate dissociation are important, but unfortunately they bypass the essential point, namely, the assumption of two noncompatible, conflicting psychic systems, and the inevitable distortion of mental contents which occurs upon passing from the first to the second system.

Janet thought that dissociation is the consequence of weakness in synthesizing. Certain experiences will become dissociated, that is, will be beyond the perimeter of awareness and out of the control of the organized personality. As a matter of fact, a theory of remembering and forgetting also has to encompass motivation, a point that Janet disregarded. However, the effects of motivation are fully comprehensible when described by a theory of consistent self and dissociated psychical realms; the self is reshaped in its totality from time to time by the impositions of circumstances. But, and here is the point, such a reshaping of the self—that is, becoming aware of previously nonretrievable remembrances—does not presuppose any distortion due to the passage from the first to the second psychic system. Availability of formerly nonretrievable memories is the function of a changed attitude, of a reorientation of the self.

In accordance with this view, Kardiner (1947) emphasized that therapeutic success with traumatic neurotics could not be attributed to the lifting of the amnesia. Rather, an amnesia of this kind is likely to improve only when "the individual's picture of the outer world has been changed, when his courage and resources in handling this new external reality had been increased or restored, at least in part" (385).

It is important to emphasize here that not all phenomena of dissociation are motivated. Breuer and Freud (1892), who thought that a "splitting of consciousness" exists in every hysteria, were careful to distinguish between two sorts of dissociation. In the first, the patient's intention causes him to forget the painful experiences and consequently not to resolve them by action or by means of associative absorption. In the second, the associative absorption fails because there is not enough associative connection between the normal state and the pathological state in which these ideas originally arose. Certain experiences are dissociated because of an opposing motive in the individual. In other cases, there are no such motives at all. Instead, the experience fails to become part of the web of the organized self, because it happens during a "hypnoid" state. Strictly speaking, only in the first case is it appropriate to speak of dissociation. The second case is, in fact, a failure in association. I would like to suggest that we revive the concept of "hypnoid" state; certain available experimental data may well encourage its use.

Overton (1964) trained rats to escape from shock in a T-maze. The adaptive response, learned while the rat was drugged with sodium pentobarbital, failed to appear if the rat was subsequently tested while not drugged; the rat had to learn the appropriate turning anew. But with the drug-conditioning reinstated, the previously learned re-

sponse was instantly available. That is, there was no transfer of learning between the drug and nondrug states, but
transfer did appear between the two drug states and between the two nondrug states. Therefore, we are led to
the conclusion that the events of different states of mind
involve separate memory systems, and that those systems
have intrinsic difficulties of communication between
them. Recall, then, is state-dependent. These separate
memory systems belong, obviously, to their respective
psychic systems, and are not interchangeable with the id
and ego systems hypothesized by Freud.

Goodwin *et al.* (1969) re-examined the question of
state-dependent recall in man. Their male subjects performed memory tasks, some while sober and others while
under the influence of alcohol. Twenty-four hours later,
they were tested under the same or different conditions.
In recall, learning transfer was better when the subject
was intoxicated during both sessions. In recognition,
transfer was not significantly affected by changing state.
Thus, alcohol appears to produce state-dependent effects
in man, though not all forms of memory are equally sensitive to it. Perhaps a controlled quantity of alcohol is not
the best means for inducing a strong form of state-
dependent effects; or, perhaps this finding depicts the real
situation—that recall is clearly influenced by a change in
the state of mind, while recognition is relatively unin-
fluenced by such a change.

These experiments on state-dependent recall vindicate
retroactively the concepts of a nonmotivated hypnoid
state and of motivated dissociation. As to the concept of
repression—it was a milestone in the history of psychology, an exciting step in the asymptotic struggle for an
understanding of behavior, but we must learn to live without it.

Primary and Secondary Processes? or States of Mind?

The concepts of repression and displacement of mental energy are inseparable from Freud's theory of psychic apparatus, and the difficulties we meet while trying to probe the concepts reflect the status of the theory. Freud conceived of the psychic apparatus as an agency for regulating and discharging mental energy, the source of which was identified as the instinctual drives. At first he divided this apparatus into systems on the basis of their relationship to consciousness: Perception-Consciousness, Preconscious, and Unconscious. Later, he became convinced of the existence of self-directed instinctual destructiveness, which led him to change his view. He suggested then that the psychic apparatus was comprised of Id-Ego systems, and that the Ego contains a further agency, the Superego. The addition of the Superego appeared to him to be necessary in order to explain the puzzles of self-punishing tendencies, especially in the obsessional and depressive states, which the earlier theory could not successfully deal with.

Freud's assumption of an instinctual drive to aggression, and the revision of the structure of psychic apparatus made necessary by it did not change his basic idea—that the psychic apparatus is one that deals with mental energy. Freud's last formulation of his theory (1938) is: "We seem to recognize that nervous or psychical energy exists in two forms . . . mobile and . . . bound; we . . . even venture to suppose . . . a synthesis in the course of which free energy is transformed into bound energy . . . we hold firmly to the view that the distinction between the unconscious and the preconscious condition also lies in dynamic relations of this kind."

Mental processes of the unconscious use a mobile mental energy, and conscious processes a bound mental energy. This variation in the energy endowment causes important differences in the workings of these psychic systems. Displacement, condensation, use of symbols, loss of sense of time, or of any other feature of reality orientation characterize the processes of the first psychic system. The second system is capable of delaying discharge of energy, and obeys the rules of logic.

This distinction between primary and secondary processes is a unique feature of Freud's theory of mind. Jones (1953) was of the opinion that "Freud's revolutionary contribution to psychology was not so much his demonstrating the existence of an unconscious, and perhaps not even his exploration of its content, as his proposition that there are two fundamentally different kinds of mental processes, which he termed primary and secondary, respectively" (397). Nevertheless, this thesis was not accepted unanimously even among writers influenced by Freud. Where Freud hypothesized two systems of reasoning, Silberer (1912) thought that we have one system of reasoning only, but that it has many levels of organization. When we are awake, our thinking is adapted and capable of clear conceptualization; when we are fatigued, our cognition will be only a vague approximation, an indication merely, of the intent.

In his comments on Silberer's study, Rapaport (1951) admitted that "direct evidence to decide this controversy has not been so far proffered" (218). Since the concept of primary process is one of the cornerstones of psychoanalysis, it is significant that Rapaport, one of the most influential interpreters of Freud, could not take a firm stand in regard to it. In fact, step by step Rapaport restricted the relevance of primary processes. Commenting on the work of Betlheim and Hartman (1924) on Korsakov's disease, Rapaport writes: "In our discussion of Bleuler's work on schizophrenia, we were forced to conjecture that ... many schizophrenic symptoms can be understood only if we assume that they are not referable to a specific drive or affect, but rather to a state of consciousness ..." (304). Then again: "Schilder observed mechanisms attributed to the primary process operating not only on the material of the unconscious, but also on the fringe of consciousness. ... It seems that Bleuler's concept of 'autistic thinking' may also have had its origin in similar observations. The mechanism of the primary process may not be as exclusive to the unconscious as has been thought" (502).

Unfortunately, Rapaport did not follow his own ideas to their final conclusion. It is embarrassing to see him maintaining that there are two psychical systems regulated by different motives, with diametrically opposed ways of working, while at the same time admitting the possibility that the "mechanisms attributed to the primary process" operate not only in the first psychical system, but also on material on the fringe of consciousness. Rapaport was aware that concepts like fringe of consciousness and autistic thinking are the real alternatives to the concept of primary-secondary process. James, Kuelpe, Schilder, and Bleuler, as well as Freud, dealt with these same phenomena, but only Freud postulated two dynamically interacting systems of reasoning. After all his concessions, Rapaport might well have wondered what remained of Freud's original proposition. Instead, he suggested that there are "mechanisms of primary process' which define the first psychical system, and also there are "mechanisms of primary process"—the same mechanisms—which do *not* define the first psychical system.

Besides, Freud could not accept the revision put forward by Rapaport. Freud's approach (1900) was:

> All that I insist upon is the idea that the activity of the *first* system is directed towards securing the *free discharge* of the quantities of excitation, while the *second* system, by means of the cathexes emanating from it, succeeds in *inhibiting* this discharge and in transforming the cathexis into a quiescent one, no doubt with a simultaneous raising of its potential. I presume, therefore, that under the dominion of the second system the discharge of excitation is governed by quite different mechanical conditions from those in force under the dominion of the first system (59).

These are clear words; nevertheless, his translator, Strachey, in an effort to emphasize the importance of this formulation, inserted a footnote of his own reminding the reader that, "The distinction between the primary and secondary systems, and the hypothesis that psychical functioning operates differently in them, are among the most fundamental of Freud's concepts" (1900, 601).

These sentences speak for themselves. Rapaport's revision is incompatible with Freud's idea because Freud envisioned a dichotomy, whereas Rapaport would have preferred a continuum. For, although it is formulated cautiously, this is the meaning of Rapaport's proposition about the appearance of primary processes on the fringe of consciousness. Freud's model of the mental apparatus —two psychical systems, the censorship upon the passage from one of them to the other, the inhibition and overlaying of one activity by the other, the relations of both to consciousness—is only conceivable as a constant clash between systems whose functioning is completely different.

To point out the differences between fringe and focus of consciousness, as Rapaport did, is only a small step from acknowledging the nonsequitur of Freud's theory of behavior. That was not Rapaport's intention; quite the contrary. Unintentionally, however, while doing his best to reconcile the inherent difficulties of Freud's theory, Rapaport made it apparent that the concept of primary process, of a psychic system which has no adaptive function and no reality-oriented cognition, is hardly defendable even by devoted theoreticians of psychoanalysis.

As Jones (1953, I, 365) points out, at the base of Freud's view concerning the mental apparatus apparently lie the "mental mechanics" formulated by Herbart. Herbart (1825) thought that psychic life consists of a continuing interaction between ideas of varying intensity. As a result of this interaction, one idea may arrest another. No idea is destroyed by this inhibition; it merely passes from a state of reality to a state of potential. However, the inhibited idea will not pass back from a state of tendency to a state of reality unless it succeeds in overcoming an obstacle, a *limen* (threshold) of consciousness.

As a highschool student, Freud studied psychology from a Herbartian textbook and learned then about the concept of a limen. The great Fechner also influenced Freud's thinking here. Fechner demonstrated experimentally the existence of a threshold of consciousness by showing that just noted differences (jnd) between stimuli do not immediately reflect outer changes; rather, our sensations increase in proportion to the logarithm of the stimulus. That is, the sensation must gain a certain amount of intensity before it can be consciously registered. Weber-Fechner's law made apparent the existence of a psychic structure, or at least of a demarcation line, a thresh-

old, the overleaping of which is essential before a thing
can be consciously perceived. Weber-Fechner's law also
supported Herbart's ideas about the mental mechanics of
inhibition, and the incessant striving of ideas to enter
consciousness.

Herbart's concept of a limen seems to be a well-established and enduring contribution to psychology. Lashley
(1951) points out that many activities require for their
performance both a specific patterning and also a general
facilitation, a rise in dynamic level. According to his analysis, hemiplegia and motor aphasia are primarily expressions of a low level of facilitation, rather than a loss of the
specific integrative connections that are involved in the
use of language or in the patterning of our movements. A
monkey, for example, after ablation of the precentral
gyrus may seem unable to use its arm at all; but if its
emotional excitement is raised above a certain level, the
arm is freely used. As soon as the excitement dies down,
the arm is again hemiplegic. Therefore, concludes Lashley, "The problem of the availability of memories ... may
find a partial solution in such fluctuations in a dynamic
level. In many of the organic amnesias the pattern of
integration seems to be retained but can be motivated
only by an abnormally intense sensory or central rein-
forcement" (124).

Freud would agree with Lashley's reasoning as far as
organic amnesias are considered. In the analysis of nonor-
ganic amnesias, however, Freud went further in two directions: he hypothesized two psychic systems that work
differently, and he also hypothesized a hostile interaction
between them—that is, a struggle between drive and defense. The idea of defense against stimuli was perhaps
suggested by the psychophysical equation of Fechner.

The fact that differences between stimuli are only perceived after this span is appropriately augmented may be understood as a reluctance to yield to stimuli, as an attempt to build a barrier against them. Indeed, Freud (1921) did his best to depict the possible dangers of an unhampered flux of stimuli: "This little fragment of living substance is suspended in the middle of an external world charged with the most powerful energies; and it would be killed by the stimulation emanating from there if it were not provided with a protective shield against stimuli. . . . its outermost surface . . . becomes to some degree inorganic and thenceforward functions as a special envelope or membrane resistant to stimuli . . . *Protection against* stimuli is an almost more important function for the living organism than *reception of stimuli*" (26).

The need of defending oneself against stimuli explains ". . . why speaking anatomically, consciousness should be lodged on the surface of the brain instead of being safely housed somewhere in its innermost interior" (1921, 24). The perceptual system and its subjective aspect, consciousness, function as a sentinel; accordingly, they are placed at the gate.

As is known today, but was not in Freud's time, the propagation of stimuli is a twofold matter: specific, to the corresponding cortical sensory area; and nonspecific, to the arousal system (RAS). Sensory excitations may reach the sensory projection areas, but the loop circuits which appear to be the main basis of cortical transmission do not function unless the arousal system is providing a sort of general summation to all cortical synapses. It is this arousal system which is mainly responsible for consciousness and for regulating the quantity and intensity of perceived stimuli. However, it is sited subcortically, and not on the surface of the brain. Despite this necessary revision of Freud's speculation, these new developments in our knowledge do not necessarily negate the assumption of a stimulus barrier. What does make it questionable, however, is the information obtained by sensory deprivation experiments.

These experiments revealed the extent to which we depend on receiving stimulation. Contrary to what Freud (and Fechner) thought, it is now plain that being deprived of stimuli is anything but the ideal condition for existence. The mental functioning of subjects sensorily deprived very soon deteriorates: they are not able to think coherently, they suffer from hallucinations, and their body images and psychic identities are in danger of disintegration. Instead of saying that protection against stimuli is almost more important than reception of stimuli, we have to say, in fact, that normal functioning is made possible only by bombardment by stimuli. Nevertheless, we do not have to give up the concept of a limen. The question only is whether we have to interpret it as a defensive device against outer and inner stimuli. Other interpretations are also possible.

In an astonishingly modern approach, Bergson (1901, 1902) suggested a theory of mental functioning, at the center of which is a concept of mental effort, apparently one of the spiritual children of Herbart's limen. The concept of mental effort has two main components. First, it emphasizes the constructive, active aspect of perception and remembering. It was Bergson's opinion that perception is anything but a faithful copy of stimuli. Rather, perception is the end product of an interpretative process, whereby some stimuli serving as cues arouse memories, and the mutual adaptation between them results in what we perceive. If we read every letter, we would not be able to read as much as we do. What we do instead is utilize only segments of a written text, and thereby quicken our reading. That is to say, reading is a constructive activity rather than a passively received impression. The description of this constructive activity is the second component of the concept of mental effort. In Bergson's view, the mental activity of perceiving and remembering is a process of unfolding; it begins with a dynamic scheme and ends up with the retrieval of the sought-for individual idea.

This scheme is neither a picture nor an abstraction, but an outline of directions; this is why it is a dynamic scheme. The "tip of the tongue" phenomenon is perhaps the paradigm of this process. Bergson illustrates it by citing the fact that while preparing a list of authors, he arrived at one whose contribution to the topic he remembered well, but whose name, nevertheless, he was unable to remember. In trying to recall it, at first, he had a feeling about some barbaric, bestial deed. The verb *prendre* and the name *Arbogast*, from the ancient history of Rome, came to mind. Bergson thought about Arbogast's barbaric deeds. Then the characters *d* and *r* became noticeable; and as it turned out, the sought-for name was Prendergast. This is how we proceed from the dynamic scheme to the individual word. The scheme delineates the area of searching and also immediately stresses certain properties. This becomes very clear in a recent work by Brown and McNeill (1966) on this "tip of the tongue" phenomenon. Unable to recall the name of the street on which a relative lived, one subject thought of *Congress* and *Corinth* and *Concord*. The words that had come to mind here have certain properties in common with the target word:

all four begin with *Co,* all are two-syllable words, all put primary stress on the first syllable.

Perceiving and remembering by means of dynamic schemes obviously are made possible only by an investigating effort. An associational model allows one perhaps to envisage psychic life as a stimulus-governed, effortless stream. The model of a dynamic scheme, on the other hand, is unthinkable without the assumption of an effort, a mental effort. The "tip of the tongue" attests to the fact that active strategies of matching and mismatching occur before the identity of an individual idea is established. However, there are differences during the different states of consciousness as to the capability of mobilizing mental effort. When relaxed or uninterested in his surroundings, an individual's mental effort will not be strong enough to evolve the sought-for ideas from their schemes. Consequently, the product of cognition will be unusual or even bizarre compared with controlled waking thoughts, like Arbogast instead of Prendergast; it becomes even more unusual if one ends up by recollecting stories of violence instead of the name of an author.

The difference between Bergson's view and Freud's mental apparatus is that the theory of unfolding from a dynamic scheme does not demand the assumption of two different psychic systems. The mental products which Freud sees as evidence of primary process are explained by Bergson as the consequences of a lowered mental effort. Again we have to ask—primary-secondary processes, or states of mind? Let us examine some evidence that supports Bergson, Silberer, and others who envisaged a single psychic system.

Microgenesis

Although it is reasonable to think that the dynamic scheme unfolds in a stepwise development, Bergson did not follow up the implications of this thought. However, Sander (1928) proposed a theory of perception which may be regarded as complementary to Bergson's. Sander conducted his experiments by presenting visual stimuli very briefly in a tachistoscope, in dim light, in indirect view, or in extreme miniature; then he gradually improved these unfavorable conditions. He was able to show that unfavorable to normal circumstances give rise to a whole series of perceptual experiences, thus displaying the evolution of the final gestalt in logical order. For this process of gradual configuration, Sander suggested the term *Aktualgenese*, which Werner (1956) translated as *microgenesis*.

The theory of microgenesis contains two theses, one referring to the emergence of a percept, and the other to the accompanying subjective experiences. Under the unfavorable conditions mentioned above, the first stage of an evolving gestalt is an undifferentiated "fog of light" (*Helligkeitenebel* as Undeutsch called it, 1942), a mere impression of hue the boundaries of which cannot be defined. The next stage is a ground figure differentiation, the inner area demarcated by a clear, mostly round line, although its contents remain vague and amorphous. After this, the contour and inner content became more distinct, but this configuration is very unstable and changing. Then arises the first real gestalt: the previous "skeletal" gestalt is completed with elaborations and modifications. Now, a surprise—just before the final gestalt, the percept again becomes labile, and its inner area loses its former articulateness; it is more simple and regular in form and content than the final form which follows it. This stage is the *Vorgestalt*. Only after that does the complete, articulated, elaborated (and categorized) percept appear.

The formation of the successive stages, following each other by sudden jerks, has a certain shading of nonfinality; the intermediate stages lack the relative stability and composure of the final forms; they are restless, agitated, and full of tensions, as though in a fluid state of becoming. Thus, a contour, which according to the actual stimulus is interrupted, is perceived accordingly but then tends to close again at the next movement, only to open once more. To get a percept one may sometimes experience a story drama.

As to the microgenesis of thought, two major tenets are emphasized: 1) Concepts evolve afresh on every occasion from a dynamic scheme, running through such different stages as clang associations, contaminations and analogies, and sometimes swinging persistently between superficial and meaningful associations; 2) A disturbance of this process, or an inability to push the process to its anticipated goal will lead to premature closure of the cognition at one of the stages of the normal development of thought.

I shall quote here part of a conversation between an aphasic patient and his doctor which will demonstrate this point. The interest of the authors here (Ross *et al.*, 1964) was a linguistic one; the interpretations given after are mine.

(38) *D:* Is your speech back to normal yet?
     P: Hear? Yes, definitely.
(39) *D:* Your speaking?
     P: Speaking? Yes, yes.
(40) *D:* It's quite back to normal?

P: *Yes, yes.*

(41) D: Nothing wrong with it at all?

P: *No, nothing whatever.*

(42) D: You don't get mixed up sometimes?

P: *No, no.*

(43) D: Good.

P: *No, my lunging's perfect.*

(44) D: Your what's perfect?

P: *My lunging.*

(45) D: Your lunging?

P: *Longing, yes, my longing to you; to—to the story is perfect. I understand, I—er—I get everything that I understand. I know.*

(46) D: M'm, I see.

P: *But whenever there is English between us— language, anything like that. I—I'm perfect. I can tell you that, definite.*

(47) D: Yes.

P: *Without any t-touch.*

(48) D: M'm.

P: *I've—I'm very good. I've had a good education.*

(49) D: Yes.

P: *No, I'm not admitting tale to you, sir, you, or any man your level.*

(50) D: M'm.

P: *I'll easy hold my own.*

(51) D: Yes.

P: *I've got a very good luggage.*

(52) D: M'm. Now that's not quite the right word, is it? Not *luggage.*

P: *Well—*

(53) D: What's the word you were trying to think of?

> P: *Oh, good language, then.*
> (54) D: Ah, that's better.
>   P: *Language. I—I'm saying now lot—roughly—*
>   *I'm saying to you, luggage. I—I'm speaking*
>   *language; I—I'm very good.*
> (55) D: M'm.
>   P: *I've got a good language.*

We have here an opportunity to follow the major steps of the microgenesis of the word "language." Fortunately, both participants of this conversation were interested in achieving the elusive word.

During the dialogue the patient makes notable efforts to get the word; meanwhile, we glimpse the evolving of a word, which normally cannot be observed. On the first occasion, not quoted here, he says: "I shall have lesson with the lungage of the hear itself." Later, "It'll underneath—underneath my *luggage* that's got my upper ha—er—the worst hand to me." In dialogue 43, "No, my lunging's perfect"; dialogue 45, *"Longing,* yes my *longing* to you—to the story is perfect." Then, suddenly (dialogue 46), "But whenever there is English between us—*language,* anything like that, I—I'm perfect. I can tell you that, definite." After this comes a retreat (the to-and-fro oscillation): "I've got a very good *luggage.* " which is followed by, in dialogue 53: "Oh, good *language* then; "repeating it with great affect in dialogue 54: "I—I'm saying now lot—roughly—I'm saying to you, *luggage.* I—I'm speaking *language;* I—I'm very good.

The order of the spoken words was *lungage—luggage —lunging—longing—language—luggage—language— luggage—language.* We can see that the critical point was the vowel: *lu-* through three trials; *lo-; la-.* After this came the oscillation between *language* and *luggage*, and only then was the concept stabilized. It is possible that the patient had many more intermediate associations, but perhaps because of his intense goal-directedness, his awareness of being examined, and as it seemed to him being treated derogatorily ("I've had a good education . . . I'm not admitting tale to you, sir, or any man your level . . . I'll easy hold my own") he may have withheld some words that came to his mind. Anyway, the dialogue as it stands demonstrates the word-evolving dynamic which normally goes on rapidly and unrecognized.

The well-known protocols of experimental aphasia of Penfield and Roberts (1959) offer similar evidence. These authors produced aphasic arrest by placing stimulative electrodes at different points of the exposed cortex. Upon stimulating point 25, the patient hesitated and then correctly named the picture before him, "butterfly." Upon stimulating point 28, the patient was unable to name, as soon as the electrode was in place. The electrograph showed after discharge, which began in a nearby recording electrode and spread to involve the whole temporal region. During this, the patient continued to be unable to name and no longer answered anything. The electrographic seizure stopped suddenly and the patient spoke at once. "Now I can talk," he said. "Butterfly." When he began to talk the patient was asked why he had not been able to name the picture, and replied, "I couldn't get that word, 'butterfly' and then I tried to get the word 'moth'."

That surely was neither a motivated displacement, nor an out-of-the blue association. Had he been requested to name "moth," the patient may have been able to name "butterfly" instead—because what he temporarily suffered from was an inability to push forward the process of differentiation from the dynamic schema. Had he been able to verbalize the anticipated concept, he could have done so only after unfolding it through all the phases of microgenesis, clang associations, contaminations, analogies, perseverations, and so on. Since he suffered temporarily from an aphasic inability, he verbalized one of the preparatory phases of the target word.

Marshal and Newcombe's (1966) report of a case of selective dysphasic impairment demonstrates the validity of this statement. At first their patient suffered from complete aphasia and right hemiplegia. Slowly he improved in spontaneous speech and in the understanding of language, but not in reading and writing. The most striking and consistent feature of the patient's language impairment was the occurrence of paralexic errors. The patient read *antique* as *vase, canary* as *parrot, liberty* as *freedom*. Sometimes the stimulus word was completed, though unnecessarily: *beg* was read as *beggar*. *For, me, before, up,* and other words were all read as *and*. Two findings of this study are especially pertinent here. First is that the authors point out the impossibility of the patient having motor (articulatory) difficulties with those words he failed to read correctly. "There are many examples where he produced [in another context] a word which he had read erroneously (e.g., THUNDER read as storm and STORM read as thunder). The disturbance is clearly more a central than an articulatory difficulty."

Precisely so. The central difficulty referred to here is the self-same premature closure of microgenesis I have assumed earlier regarding *butterfly* and *moth* in the protocol of Penfield and Roberts. The same word which was nonretrievable as the target word was available as one of the preparatory phases of another word. That is, what these patients suffered from was not a loss of words (a view held also by Lashley, as we have seen), but rather, a failure in pushing the microgenesis to its final point. The report of Marshal and Newcombe contains a second important point. They observed their patient making an effort to retrieve the correct word in a peculiar way. As the word *agent* was to be read, the patient answered "Not a spy, a firm's—". Given the word *college*, he responded "School . . . not ordinary." *Canal* was replied "Not river . . . small river." Such negations also appear in the protocol published by Ross *et al.* (1964). The doctor asks, "Could you tell me again what your job is?" The patient answers: "I'm not—er—the head man; I—I'm d-deputy man."

These negations seem to me to be the step nearest to reaching the right answer. The inhibition of *spy*, for example, was the last obstacle before the closure of the thought development: a firm's agent. Significantly, medical patients who are recovering from anaesthesia—so I am informed by a nurse who works with them—often formulate their requests by negation, instead of positively. It goes without saying that negation, as one of the phases of the microgenesis of concepts, has nothing to do with negativism. Indeed, Rapaport (1951) remarked that association by negation and contrast are suggestive of relatively well-preserved paranoic cases. Those cases need not clinically show any obvious and striking negativistic symptoms.

We may say, then, that the microgenetic approach deals successfully with the process of cognition, providing a unified theory of perception and reasoning. Without hypothesizing two systems of reasoning, it explains both reality-adapted and disturbed performances. The process of unfolding the dynamic scheme is usually not observable. However, endopsychic conflicts, relaxation, fatigue, distraction, sleep, altered states of consciousness, or organic diseases may disturb the microgenesis of concepts, and cause its premature closure at one of the preparatory phases. Dreamy mentation, as well as thought disturbances, are mentations produced under such circumstances. We do not yet know the exact serial order of these phases, though we can say that they involve clang-associations, condensations, analogues, symbols, opposites, and their negations. The process is not straightforward; it rather often perseveres, and swings between approaching and relapsing from the target word.

I would like to emphasize again that we have only one neuropsychological system subserving states of mind. Pondering this problem from the neurophysiological point of view, Galambos warns against the popular inclination to conceive of the levels of the brain as higher and lower, in a kind of order with the cerebral cortex on top. Instead, Galambos points out, the neuronal organization responsible for certain behavior is essentially longitudinal, running from front to back in the brain. For instance, vomiting can be caused by administering shocks to localized areas of the paleocortex, hypothalamus, and medulla. Therefore, Galambos concludes, "the neural organizations responsible for the response are equal at several different 'levels'. . . . Whatever the 'higher' level imposes upon the 'lower' one is unimportant compared to the fact that all are involved in producing the act" (1961, 652).

Anokhin is of the opinion that, "At the present time one can hardly maintain that the process of learning is the exclusive prerogative of any one nervous structure, the cortex or subcortex. . . . all these component parts of the brain functioning at a given moment are jointly involved in this dynamic activation" (1961, 150).

Thus, we have states of mind, but only one system of mental functioning.

Etiology of neuroses—the unsolved problem

Have symptoms a hidden meaning? If it is impossible to prove repression, displacement, and primary and secondary processes, how can we substantiate Freud's (1939) assertion that the symptoms of neuroses are "without exception" either a substitutive satisfaction of some sexual urge or measures to prevent such a satisfaction, and that as a rule they are compromises between the two? The sexual origin of neurotic symptoms, said Freud, should not immediately be apparent; the erotic and destructive components are interpenetrating, and the decision to which of them to assign the responsibility may not be easy. Nevertheless, Freud thought that, "There is no doubt that sexual instincts play a prominent, unexpectedly large part in the causation of the neuroses."

This explicit commitment to the psychosexual etiology of all the neurotic disturbances, however, was never realizable because of the puzzle of traumatic neurosis: it was not possible to find any connection between the post-traumatic state and infantile sexuality (Freud, 1939). In fact, Freud's assumption also does not fit obsessive-compulsive neurosis.

Ever since Westphal (1878) defined the obsessional state, the urge to think or to do a certain thing and yet to be repelled by it has been considered its singular characteristic. Janet (1903) stressed also the features of indecision, checking, hesitancy, and a tendency to introspection and to depersonalization. While these phenomena are drastic enough to be experienced by the subject as the essence of the disturbance, the observer may be impressed by the rituals associated with obsessional states. Lewis (1936), however, cautioned against such a view. He was of the opinion that such rituals are secondary manifestations only, and the core of the disturbance is the conflict between a compulsion and the resistance to it. Unless this warning is taken seriously, one has difficulty in accounting for the rituals of animals which, on the surface, look like the symptoms of human neuroses.

In the experimental neuroses studied by Masserman (1961), one animal developed the ritual of circling the foodbox three times and bowing on its forepaws before attempting to feed. As another example, in one of his experiments on the effects of early experiences upon later behavior, Melzack (1965) compared normally raised dogs with dogs raised in a severely restricted environment. They had to learn to press a window in order to get food. The restricted dogs easily learned the task; they performed it, however, in a curiously stereotyped manner. One of the restricted dogs turned a complete circle before each press on the window and again before eating the food. This response pattern disappeared slowly over a five-day period. Another restricted dog licked the slice of meat as soon as it landed in the cage, pulled it around the cage, rubbed her head against it, and finally left it in a corner. She pressed the window again and repeated the same pattern until she collected one to two dozen slices. Only then did she eat them voraciously, sometimes regurgitating and re-eating them.

Stereotyped behavior patterns like these were never observed in the control dogs in the window-pressing experiment. They were, however, observed in one of the control dogs during a visual discrimination test. During training for discrimination between a horizontal and a vertical line, one of the normal control dogs became indistinguishable from the restricted dogs. He showed an increasingly high level of excitement, and struggled violently when he was picked up. At the same time he developed a strong position habit, as well as stereotyped behavior patterns such as turning two complete circles before responding to the stimuli. Concomitantly, his error scores shifted into the range of the restricted dogs.

It is hard to imagine how one can explain the rituals of these animals as substitute instinctual satisfaction—that is, in terms of drive, instead of cognitive theory. It is rather obvious that in the discrimination training something happened that was fairly similar to what happened in Pavlov's experiment. In the case of human neurotics, however, I assume we would feel no great difficulty in discovering the "hidden" symbolic meanings of such rituals. But if we are not constricted by human racism, we will be ready to consider the possibility of similar causations for similar phenomena in man and animal.

At any rate, in cases where it is possible to identify the genesis of a ritual in an animal, and then follow it up, one may be impressed, as Lorenz (1963) puts it, by the similarity of the basic function of a habit in a goose and in the cultural development of sacred rites in man. The observation made by Lorenz is as follows: he reared a greylag goose from the egg. When the goose, Martina by name, was about a week old, he let her walk upstairs to his bedroom. As Martina, following him, walked into the hall, she was suddenly struck by terror, and tried, as frightened birds always do, to reach the light. She ran from the door straight toward the window, passing Lorenz where he stood on the bottom stair. At the window, she waited a few moments to calm down, then she came to him on the step and followed him up to the bedroom.

This procedure was repeated in the same way the next evening, except that this time her detour to the window was a little shorter and she did not remain there so long. The habitual detour to the window became shorter and shorter; after a year there remained of the whole path habit only a right-angled turn.

One evening Lorenz forgot to let Martina in. When he finally opened the door, the anxious goose, contrary to her usual custom, ran directly to the stairs—choosing the shortest route, skipping her usual right-angle turn, and starting immediately to climb the stairs. Upon this, Lorenz reports, "something shattering happened. Arrived at the fifth step, she suddenly stopped, made a long neck, in geese a sign of fear, and spread her wings as for flight. Then she uttered a warning cry and very nearly took off. Now she hesitated a moment, turned round, ran hurriedly down the five steps and set forth resolutely like someone on a very important mission, on her original path to the window and back. This time she mounted the steps according to her former custom from the left side. On the fifth step she stopped again, looked round, shook herself and greeted, behaviour mechanisms regularly seen in greylags when anxious tension has given place to relief. I hardly believed my eyes" (1963, 58).

An instructive observation indeed, demonstrating the strength of habit. Once acquired, the goose could not break it without being stricken by fear. Man, too, may be subject to similar traumatic experiences. One cannot take for granted that rituals are, by definition, defensive devices against warded-off impulses, unless one is ready to assume a similar conflict in the goose.

On the other hand, a clash between will and compulsion, pointed out by Lewis as the core phenomenon of the obsessional states, is only possible in a creature capable of self-reflection. Freud thought that the compulsion is an attempt to compensate for an underlying trouble, the doubt. "The *doubt* corresponds to the patient's internal perception of his own indecision, which in consequence of the inhibition of his love by his hatred, takes possession of him in the face of every intended action. The doubt is in reality a doubt of his own love . . . and it becomes diffused over everything else, and is especially apt to become displaced on to what is most insignificant and small. A man who doubts his own love, may, or rather *must,* doubt every lesser thing" (1909, 241).

Freud assumes here that a regression to the ambivalent-anal stage of libido development is responsible for an ongoing doubt about whether one loves or hates; and this doubt is compensated for by a compulsion. However, this assumption is less than self-evident. It appears to be a biased attempt to establish a causal connection between psychosexuality and compulsion, rather than to account for the facts. To doubt one's ability to love does not inevitably lead to an incessant uncertainty over whether the address was correctly written or the windows closed. But even granting such a pervasive generalization, this assumption must deal with another difficulty: does regression make inevitable the emergence of doubts? Young children are able to shift their emotions quickly; they may love and hate in quick succession, and without suffering from incapacitating doubts. Why, then, should the obsessive patient, if he is, indeed, regressed, be vexed by doubts?

Still, one may perhaps rescue the drive theory of the

obsessive-compulsive neurosis by agreeing that the compulsion indicates the pressure of a drive, aggression, rather than the compensation of a doubt. The aggressive drive elicits the defensive maneuvers of the ego system, and their undecided battle ends up in a maladaptive compromise, the obsessive-compulsive neurosis. Such a view would do justice to Freud's revised theory of mind, which assumes two basic drives of Eros and Thanatos. But this turnabout would require giving up the concept of regression, because the preoccupation with hostile impulses would now be evidence of the primary aggression, rather than of a retreat to an earlier, anal phase. Also, the statement that neurotic symptoms are, without exception, a substitute satisfaction for some sexual urge would have to be amended as regards the obsessional (and the post-traumatic) states.

An observation emphasized mainly by British psychiatrists, namely, the coincidence of depression with obsessional states, may support this idea about aggression. In recent research, Mellett (1974) concluded that "Depression is *always* present at the onset of obsessional symptoms, when these are of pathological degree." For example, he cites one female patient's symptoms. She had an irresistible belief that if food had been, to her direct knowledge, touched by others it might be harmful, and that if she cooked food, those eating it would become blind or drop dead. Also, when she was driving with her husband in his car, she felt compelled to add up the numbers of various cars they passed. All these symptoms began with puerperal depression, which became chronic and was reinforced by the death of an exasperating mother-in-law.

The symptoms of another of Mellett's patients included

the fear that she would be contaminated by feces, so that she spent 30 minutes to an hour elaborately checking her clothes after using a lavatory. Her symptoms began with her separation from her stepmother; this was especially painful for her because her true mother had died when the patient was an infant.

The importance of depression in obsessional states is also suggested by the striking improvement when patients are treated with an antidepressant, even in the absence of a clinical depression (Capstick, 1971). Freud thought that at the bottom of depression lies an aggression, originally related to a love-object, but self-directed instead, resulting in cruel self-criticism; it is therefore conceivable that both the obsessional and depressive states are causally connected with the aggressive drive.

Here, however, we have to stop elaborating this idea. Depression is understood to be reaction to the loss of love, and not to the warding off of hostile impulses. Oedipal strivings originate in a pressure to allow, satisfy, or discharge an instinctual drive, but depression has nothing whatever to do with such a pressure. The experience of being abandoned is not interchangeable with a conflict between drive and defense, but rather, is to be understood in terms of object relationship.

Depression is thus a class of psychopathological phenomena which cannot be regarded as substitute satisfaction for some warded off sexual urge. Some obsessional states, on the other hand, may be explained by a conflict between the aggressive drive and defenses against it. The patient who feared to cook because food prepared by her would kill the others demonstrates such an inner psychic conflict. Fear of dirt and handwashing, on the other hand, are not related to primary aggression. If there is an instinctual need for dirt, it is not sited with the hostile impulses. If a regression to the anal-ambivalent phase is assumed, then rituals concerning cleanliness may be linked with possible hostilities. The assumption of primary aggression, however, changes this situation.

In neither case —according to the theory of regression, or according to the theory of primary aggression—can drive theory fully explain obsessional states. The stumbling block for the theory of regression is the puzzle of indecision; of primary aggression, the nonhostile compulsions, like fear of contaminating. But if Freud's suggestion turns out to be correct, that is, that the compulsion is indeed a compensation for the pain of doubts, of decision-making, then paradoxically it means he has emphasized the cognitive aspect and its centrality in psychic life.

The clash, particular to obsessional patients, between compulsion and will is reminiscent of cognitive dissonance. Festinger (1957) assumes a basic tendency in man toward consistency of cognitions. Cognitive dissonance can arise from one's awareness that one is behaving in ways which do not follow from one's beliefs, opinions, or values. The dissonance motivates behavior intended to reduce the tension. Obsessional patients, however, fail to behave according to this motive. They live under the pressure of an incessant cognitive dissonance: they are doing or thinking something contrary to their own will. It is a matter of taste whether one emphasizes the tenacity of habit or the weakness of the will; the point is, that no balance is achieved and the tension of dissonance is felt as painful.

An understanding of the conditions responsible for the inability to reduce cognitive dissonance would be the first step in explaining obsessive-compulsive neurosis. Obviously such a view is incompatible with the assumption that behavior disturbances are symbolic expressions of an unsolved, unconscious, conflict between instinctual drive and defenses. Freud's theory is especially suited to explain sexual disturbances where the assumption of a conflict between drive and inhibition is self-evident. His formulation, however, does not apply either to traumatic or to obsessive-compulsive neuroses. We do not yet know all the factors involved in the causation of neuroses; nevertheless one conclusion seems inevitable, and that is, that the mental apparatus envisaged by Freud is not the place to find them.

Chapter Four

What A Dream Is

FREUD THOUGHT that the psychodynamics of neurotic symptoms and of dreams are the same, although the dream, the *via regia* to the unconscious, is preferable for purposes of research and demonstration. It is impossible to distinguish, from the point of view of theory, between these two pillars of psychoanalytic psychology. Therefore, the statement that Freud's theory of mind is not the appropriate place to turn to explain neuroses also implies a similar point of view about his interpretation of dreams. In this chapter I shall try to show that a cognitive approach is more appropriate for dealing with these phenomena.

Freud's interpretation of dreams is not based on the manifest content of dreams, but refers to the thoughts which lie behind them. For him, the latent dream thoughts, which give the impetus to the construction of dreams, originate in the first psychical system; and that is why he said that dreams must be interpreted as wish fulfillments.

This statement is the key to psychoanalytic psychology. The theory of the mental functioning in psychopathology and of psychoanalytic treatment is a direct outgrowth of this view. The evidence for such a bold and all embracing thesis should be strong and convincing. Yet the proofs we are offered are surprisingly hesitant and evasive. Considering the possibility that conscious wishes also may generate dreams, Freud writes (1900, 552):

> *I cannot offer any proof here* that the truth is nevertheless otherwise; *but I may say that I am strongly inclined* to suppose that dream-wishes are more strictly determined. . . . I readily admit that a wishful impulse originating in the conscious will *contribute* to the instigation of a dream, but it will *probably* not do more than that.

Then again (598):

> . . . we have constructed our theory of dreams on the assumption that the dream-wish which provides the motive power invariably originates from the unconscious— *an assumption which, as I myself am ready to admit, cannot be proved to hold generally,* though, neither can it be disproved.

His main argument here is that, while it is not always possible to prove the concept of "wish," it is impossible to disprove it, and therefore his theory is valid. Years later, Popper (1961) took a similar stand. Opposing the positivist view, Popper insisted that empirical sciences may have theories. True, theories are never empirically verifiable, but they do not have to be, Popper argued; instead, they have to be testable. How? By their falsifiability, rather than by their verifiability. In other words, there is an asymmetry between verifiability and falsifiability: universal statements are never derived from singular statements, but they can be contradicted by single statements.

Using this line of reasoning, let us investigate Freud's thesis that dreams are a wish fulfillment. According to both Freud and Popper, the crucial test of a theory is whether it is falsifiable by means of a single refuting sentence.

The refutation

It is well known that Freud himself started supplying refutations of his own theory. The dreams of traumatic neurotics, monotonously repeating frightening experiences, did not fit his assumption that "the dream-wish which provides the motive power invariably originates from the unconscious." Rather, Freud suggested, this class of dream helps to carry out another task which must be accomplished before the dominance of the pleasure principle can even begin:

> These dreams are endeavoring to master the stimulus retrospectively, by developing the anxiety whose omission was the cause of the traumatic neurosis. They thus afford us a view of a function of the mental apparatus which, though it does not contradict the pleasure principle, is nevertheless independent of it and seems to be more primitive than the purpose of gaining pleasure and avoiding unpleasure (1920, 60).

Freud suggests here that the control of excitations, established stepwise by means of stereotyped repetition of overwhelming stimuli and accompanied by anxiety, developmentally precedes the unadaptive, diffuse, impulsive "discharge" of tensions (pleasure principle). Were we to accept this, we would have to deal with a tripartite mental organization. Beginning with the last, one would have the ego system functioning in accordance with reality; the id system, whose make-up enables it only to rid itself of tension; and finally, the very first system, a mental organization which precedes the "primary" one, but significantly is not even acknowledged by a name. Is it necessary that the unlabeled mental organization be superceded by the id system? After all, this "more primitive" system seems to be more helpful, biologically, than the id system, and small wonder: the pleasure principle concentrates within itself all possible oppositions to adaptation. But even if one accepts these speculations concerning the mental apparatus, the dreams of traumatic neuroses must be regarded as an instance that invalidates the assumption that the motive power of dreams is invariably a "wish."

A second instance is the punishment dream. The discussion of punishment-dreams (a paragraph added in 1911 to *The Interpretation of Dreams*) is essentially an analysis of a recurring dream of Rosegger, a famous Austrian writer who came from very humble, peasant beginnings. In one of his stories, entitled *Alienated,* Rosegger describes how he was unable for many years to free himself from the shadow of his earlier life. In his dreams he was always a journeyman tailor, working without pay in a shop. He knew well enough, in his dreams, that his right place was no longer there, but he was always sitting behind his master as his assistant. Now and then, when something went awry, he had to put up with a scolding, though there was never any talk of wages. These dreams persisted for years with uncanny regularity. Then, in one of these dreams, another journeyman was taken on, but there was no more room for another seat. The master said to Rosegger, "You've no gift for tailoring, you can go! You're alienated." Rosegger awoke feeling an overpowering fright, but from that night on he enjoyed peace. He dreamed no more of the tailoring days, he was alienated. Being alienated is, certainly, not the greatest blessing, but Rosegger was satisfied, and he was consciously satisfied for many years. What he achieved, he could now feel, was no more than confirmation of the existing facts.

Freud agreed that this class of dreams "offers a hard test to the theory of wish-fulfillment." These are punishment dreams of a parvenu, he suggested. They remind the dreamer, who is inclined to boast, of his humble origins. "The essential characteristic of punishment-dreams would thus be that in their case the dream-constructing wish is not an unconscious wish derived from the repressed . . . but a punitive one reacting against it and belonging to the ego . . ." (1954, 558).

While it tries to solve one riddle, this explanation creates many more. It is rather surprising to learn that the dreamer's inclination to boast is a repressed wish and that it arouses a punitive reaction—while dreaming. As a matter of fact, Rosegger was proud of being a successful writer, and he did not need displacement or symbolizations to experience his joy and pride. Furthermore, in his dreams Rosegger sat in the tailor shop with resistance, and thought of giving notice and taking his leave. He insisted that his rightful place was no longer there, and eventually he gained his freedom—by alienation. It does not seem as though he was being punished by self-criticism in his dreams. Instead, the opposite occurred. His daytime successes had to convince the dreaming Rosegger that he was well and alive, and not in danger of being pushed back to his earlier existence. These dreams remind us of the repetitive dreams of traumatic neuroses; the question thus arises whether punishment dreams are, indeed, a separate category.

In any case, neither the dreams of traumatic neurosis nor the punishment dreams are consistent with Freud's statement that, "We have accepted the idea that the reason why dreams are invariably wish-fulfillments is that they are products of the system whose activity knows no other aim than the fulfillment of wishes and which has at its command no other forces than wishful impulses . . ." (1954, 568). Is it possible to state that dreams are invariably wish-fulfillments, after having written only a few pages earlier that the dream-constructing wish of punishment dreams is not an unconscious wish derived from the repressed? And is it possible to agree that the dreams of traumatic neurotics are not wish fulfillments, and at the same time to base the assumption that dreams are invariably wish fulfillments upon the impossibility of disproving that they are?

These two instances supplied by Freud might be sufficient to disprove his theory of dreams—that is, that dreams are products of the id system and therefore by definition wish fulfillments. But there is a third piece of evidence which also refutes his theory: the dreams of psychotics.

The dreams of psychotics are, understandably, a difficult topic, but there are a few available studies that are highly relevant here. In one, done by Richardson and Moore (1963) on the manifest dream in schizophrenia, seven clinical psychiatrists and eight psychoanalysts compared specimen dreams with those of a control group of nonschizophrenic patients. They expected that schizophrenics would have much uncensored and undistorted sexual and aggressive content, "including openly revealed incestuous and primitively aggressive, sadistic, murderous, or mutilating material. . . . We may understand the panel's expectations if we recall that Freud said (1900, 567):

> . . . the fact of transference, as well as the psychoses, show us that the unconscious wishful impulses endeavor to force their way by way of the preconscious system into consciousness and to obtain control of the power of movement.

Accordingly, the judges expected that the dreams of schizophrenics, compared to the nonschizophrenics, would reveal less distortion, less censorship; that id wishes would appear, so to speak, nakedly. What they found, however, was that undisguised primitively aggressive dreams (including bodily mutilation) and undistorted sexual dreams (including incest) occurred with no more frequency in the schizophrenics than in the nonschizophrenic group. "In other words . . . repression (i.e., censorship) appeared to be approximately as effective in the dream of the schizophrenic as in the nonschizophrenic." Significantly, the second expectation of the judges was correct: the dreams of schizophrenics had a quality of bizarreness, uncanniness, unreality, strangeness, or cosmicality. These characteristics were the elements that most clearly differentiated the two groups.

That left these experts with two possibilities: to reconsider the psychoanalytic theory of schizophrenia, or to constrict the range of the concept of the wish. They chose the second possibility, and like Freud dealing with the traumatic neurosis, they wonder, "Does the dream serve a different function in the schizophrenic than the wish-fulfillment function?"

What they seem to forget, however, is that the dream is the most important proof of psychoanalytic psychology. Every manipulation of the thesis of dream wish fulfillment has an immediate impact on the entire structure of psychoanalysis. If dreams are not invariably motivated from the unconscious id, then behavior, normal as well as abnormal, can not be said to be invariably rooted in it. It is not possible to diminish step by step the generality of the wish fulfillment of dreams, and at the same time to deal with the pleasure principle as if nothing had happened.

Freud considered the hypothesis of the existence of two psychical systems endowed with different means of regulation inevitable due to the evidence obtained by dream analysis. If, however, the traumatic/punishment dream, and the dreams of schizophrenics are not fulfillment of repressed wishes, then, according to the principle of falsifiability proposed by Freud and Popper, the wish fulfillment theory of dreams is disproved. But then the concepts of pleasure principle, mental apparatus, primary and secondary processes, the assumption that symptoms are substitute satisfactions of the sexual urge, and so on, lose their main support.

Summarizing the findings of his inquiry, Freud (1900) stated that the "motive force [of dreams] is in every instance a wish seeking fulfillment; the fact of their not being recognizable as wishes and their many peculiarities and absurdities are due to the influence of the psychical censorship to which they have been subjected during the process of their formation" (533). This psychical censorship, which is one of the functions of the ego system, bars dream thoughts from the path to consciousness during the day. During the night these thoughts—that is, wishes—are able to obtain access to consciousness, but distortedly, and in a disguised form. Even while sleeping, censorship does not cease to function.

Although the formulation is binding and does not leave room for any concession ("The motive force is in every instance a wish seeking fulfillment"), Freud also tells us that the punishment dream does not fit the wish fulfillment theory. Punishment dreams "must be reckoned as belonging not to the repressed but to the 'ego' . . . Thus punishment-dreams indicate the possibility that the ego may have a greater share than was supposed in the construction of dreams" (1900, 558). This evasive sentence amounts to adding a question mark after the binding formulation.

Dreams which do not originate in repressed wishes do not, so to speak, need to deceive censorship: their dream-constructing thought is not in conflict with the ego system. We may thus expect punishment dreams to differ in their make-up from the usual dreams. Apparently neither Freud nor other psychoanalytic writers have found any such differences. As a matter of fact, it was never suggested that the need to distinguish between manifest dreams and latent (repressed) dream thoughts does not apply to the punishment dream. But if punishment dreams do differ in their origin but not in their make-up from other dreams, and if the dreams of traumatic neurotics and of psychotics do not fulfill id wishes, and if those dreams nevertheless do not differ in their characteristics from other dreams, then what remains to support the assumption that dreams are a disguised expression of repressed wishes?

The continuum of defence

I would like to suggest a further way of testing the suppressed wish assumption and its corollary, the inevitably ongoing conflict between drive and defence—namely, by comparing the dreams of a subject with his own day dreams. Day dreams were not extensively dealt with by Freud; nevertheless, in general we know his opinion about them:

> Like dreams [daytime phantasics] are wish-fulfillments; like dreams, they are based to a great extent on impressions of infantile experience; like dreams, they benefit from a certain degree of relaxation of censorship (1900, 492).

Daydreams as well as dreams originate in the unconscious id wishes. But there is a difference of degree between them with regard to their final organization. Due to the waking organization of the ego system, daydreams must be more censored, more disguised, than night dreams; they stand at the midpoint between dreams and controlled thinking. The best way to prove the existence of such a continuum would be to compare the dreams and daydreams of someone who is struggling with a well-defined conflict. If his daydreams faintly express, as expected, the conflicting wish, and his dreams do the same more emphatically, we would have positive proof of the concept of wish and defence. Actually, a success or failure in proving the continuum of dreams—daydreams—controlled thinking might be regarded as a most important test of Freud's theory of the pleasure principle and mental organization.

Ford and Urban (1963) reported a pertinent case. A

young man was repeatedly disturbed by fearful dreams which he felt to be "inescapable indications" of homosexuality and of aggressive-sadistic impulses toward his mother. He awakened from these recurring dreams in great panic, and remained confused about the reality of the events of the dream. In addition, his waking hours were disturbed by alarming experiences in which he had the feeling that people were inserting penises into his rectum. He described his attempts to resist the sensation, to deny its existence, but the sensation persisted to such a degree that he felt forced to admit he felt it. If he accidentally brushed up against another man, he was terrified that either he would insert his penis into the man's rectum or receive the man's penis into his. He was unable to say which was more likely.

This patient indulged in homosexual fantasies while awake, but in his dreams the same wish was expressed rather circumstantially. This is scarcely evidence of a censorship relaxed in sleep. The same experience, the homosexual wish, which during the day elicited a rather positive, participating attitude, caused terror when it occurred in his dreams. We would expect the opposite to be true, namely, that anxiety would grow in direct relationship to the increasingly straightforward expressions of an id wish. Thus, instead of demonstrating an ever-stronger influence of censorship from dreams through daydreams to directed thinking, this example rather suggests something else.

From my own experience, I can confirm Ford and Urban's finding. I also treated a young male patient troubled by homosexual panic, who indulged in homosexual fantasies while preparing himself to sleep; however, their slightest indication in dreams woke him with terror. This puzzling circumstance led me to compare, experimentally, dreams with other contemporaneous mentations of the same subject.

Nine women, aged 20–40, were the subjects of the first experiment. All of them lived in a small agricultural community; the experimenter, a student of mine, also lived in the same village. They were first given the Thematic Apperception Test (TAT); then they were asked to write down over a period of five months every dream they were able to recall. By the end of this time, we obtained from each volunteer an average of 17 TAT stories and 4.5 dreams. Both the dreams and TAT stories were analyzed according to the scoring system of Hall and VanDeCastle (1966), based on factors of characters, social interactions, achievement outcome, environmental press, emotions, settings, familiarity, and so on. We restricted our comparison to the analysis of characters, emotions, and aggressive interactions.

Both in TAT stories and dreams the majority of characters were female. Among the emotions (worry, sadness, anger, and happiness), the only statistically significant difference found was the more frequent occurrence of sadness in TAT stories. The finding relevant to our discussion here compares aggressive interactions in both these mentations. (See Table 1, page 88.)

Using the scale of Hall and VanDeCastle, it was shown that in every subject the intensity of aggression revealed was higher in TAT stories than in dreams. That is, aggression is expressed more straightforwardly and more violently in TAT stories than in dreams. Freud's drive-defence theory assumes that in sleep the control over the instinctual drives is weakened, and becomes as loose as is possible under normal, healthy conditions. Dreams are,

TABLE 1

SOCIAL INTERACTION

Quantity and Intensity of Aggression in TAT and in Dreams

Subject	DREAM High Aggression (Physical)		Low Aggression (Verbal)		TAT High Aggression (Physical)		Low Aggression (Verbal)	
	Quantity	Intensity	Quantity	Intensity	Quantity	Intensity	Quantity	Intensity
1.	2	6	8	24	5	17	5	13
2.	2	6	5	13	0	/	6	19
3.	1	3	4	9	5	16	4	12
4.	1	2	0	/	5	11	4	9
5.	0	/	4	10	4	15	6	9
6.	1	4	0	/	2	7	0	/
7.	0	/	0	/	1	3	0	/
8.	0	/	5	23	2	8	1	4
9.	0	/	2	7	0	/	4	7

	TAT			DREAM	
	Physical Aggression	Verbal Aggression		Physical Aggression	Verbal Aggression
N	9	9		8	8
M	8.55	8.1		2.62	10.75
t	1.26			50**	

**Significant at the .01 level

therefore, the appropriate place for uncontrolled aggression to emerge. The findings of this experiment, however, reveal a situation that is the opposite of this expectation. Likewise, in a study comparing dreams with early memories, Kramer *et al.* (1971) found that while early memories contain slightly more covert than overt hostility directed outward, in dreams covert hostility directed outward is four times as common as overt hostility directed outward. I can only agree with the summation of these authors: "Any notion that the dream report reflects the unbridled expression of feelings is dispelled, we believe, by an examination of hostility in the protocols. . . . In dream reports, the indirect rather than the direct expression of hostility is clearly the preferred mode." These authors, psychoanalysts themselves, certainly did not intend to disprove Freud's thesis; indeed, they did not follow through the implications of their own findings. Nevertheless, their conclusion that in dreams, but not in early memories, the indirect expression of hostility is the preferred mode *does* disprove the wish-fulfillment theory of dreams.

Actually, I am not the first to point out the real situation displayed by a comparison of dreams and fantasies. Piaget (1946), in one of his observations describes X, at 2; 9(4) awaking with a loud scream: "It was all dark and I saw a lady over there (pointing to her bed). That's why I screamed," she explained. This lady stood with her legs apart and placed with her faeces (observation 98). The horrid lady, Piaget remarks, only did what X pretended to make her dolls or other make-believe characters do; and yet this kind of activity, which easily becomes a joke in play, is accompanied in dreams by considerable anxiety. "It would be difficult, in our opinion, not to recognize the analogy between these dreams and the games of the same children. The one difference being that in dream symbolism there are nightmares, while in ludic symbolism fear is enjoyed. . . . But as play is more easily controlled than dreams, this difference is natural enough, and the resemblances are all the more striking" (1946, 179).

This difference between fantasies and dreams, which Piaget regarded as natural, is anything but natural if viewed within the frame of reference of psychoanalysis. Kris (1952) was perhaps the only psychoanalytic writer who admitted being aware of the confusion which day dreams cause the wish fulfillment theory of dream. "The privileges of fantasy," writes Kris, "are manifold. When fantasy has taken us far enough afield, we do not, as a rule, experience shame or guilt . . . Patients may feel ashamed or guilty when reporting such fantasies, although they did not feel so while they were engaged in them, or when they recalled them. . . . Tentatively, we assume that in preoccupation with fantasy the ego withdraws cathexis from some functions of the superego" (1946, 314).

This observation of Kris is amply confirmed by the series of findings presented here. Had Kris drawn the full conclusions from his own observation, he too would have arrived at the point where Freud's theory breaks down. To assume, as Kris did, that in preoccupation with fantasy the ego "withdraws" cathexis from some functions of the superego, is no more than to reformulate factual observations in technical terms. The question to be answered is whether we can continue to work with the concept of a continuum of defenses graded from waking thought through fantasies to dreams, while at the same time pointing out that daydreams are free from censorship.

Controlled thoughts, daydreams, and dreams do not

form a continuum over which censorship is gradually relaxed. We are not ashamed or guilty while engaged in daydreams, but we may be alarmed when we dream of the same topics. Thus, it is not dreams which offer a tolerant asylum for wishes; daydreams are far more accepting and liberal in this respect. Daydreams do not demand that disguise, condensation, and clang-association appear in place of the pertinent wish; nonetheless they are able to express those wishes. What compels us, then, to undertake elaborate and ingenious distortion when we express the self-same wishes while dreaming? Plainly, the facts are incompatible with the concept of wish and the complex metastructure built upon it.

I would like to conclude by analyzing a self-observation, unbiased by any preconceived idea, of Gerard De Nerval (1956), the 19th-century French novelist who was hospitalized in a state of acute catatonic psychosis. After recovering, he wrote a book *Aurelia* (also the name of his imagined lover) which describes his experiences, fantasies, and dreams during his illness. The three dreams and three fantasies I will cite here were explicitly characterized by Nerval as being dreams and fantasies. They were all of approximately the same length.

In the first fantasy, or daydream, a friend, employing superhuman power, urges Nerval to move. The friend intends to prevent him from going to the place where death lies in wait for him. This fantasy then changes to a violent struggle between two spirits. In the second daydream, he is observing a great massacre; he sees the history of nations written in blood, with corpses of women cut to pieces by sabres. The third fantasy is about carnage and orgies, and how they periodically recur in the history of mankind.

The first dream begins with a walk in a large building. He meets a few of his former teachers and classmates there. Then he sees a spectacle. An unidentified character of uncertain gender has a fight in the clouds, until finally, he falls. He is like Dürer's Angel of Melancholy. The dreamer awakes in terror. In the second dream, he talks to someone from the other world. Then, suddenly, he notices his beloved, Aurelia. After a tiring journey through deserts and forests, he realizes that what Aurelia did was the last effort to rescue him. Alas, it came too late. She turns pale, and apparently is dying. He is awakened by his own sudden cry. In the third dream, "the divine creature of his dreams" announces the end of his mental suffering.

The dreams of this patient demonstrate what the study by Richardson and Moore also pointed out, namely, that the dreams of schizophrenics do not contain undisguised sexual or primitive aggressive material. Instead of a breakthrough of uncontrolled impulses, these dreams seem to realistically depict the dreamer's existence. They are dreams of introspection originating in the ego system rather than in the id, to use Freud's terms. Nerval's fantasies, on the other hand, do contain undistorted sadistic and orgiastic happenings.

We thus see again that the concept of a continuum of defence, of a stepwise relaxation of control over instinctual wishes, does not fit the facts. Although socially nonsanctioned wishes are, in dreams, at most faintly alluded to, in daydreams they appear with their real names. Why should we stutter in our dreams if we are able to use plain language in our daydreams? Clearly, dreams are not evoked to gratify, however distortedly, such impulses; and the characteristics of dreams are not explainable as a compromise between drive and defense.

The puzzle of unattended-to inputs

The perceived world is always articulated: there is a focus and there is a periphery, there is a figure and there is a ground, there are relevant and irrelevant stimuli. This is one of the basic facts of behavior, and a large part of psychology has been taken up with the study of how the organism advantageously selects what it should pay attention to. Surprisingly enough, dreams manage to confuse this order of things. They leave out matters that are significant while one is awake, and instead concentrate upon experiences unimportant and trivial enough to have been forgotten soon after they occurred.

Many authors who wrote about dreams before Freud were puzzled by this change in the hierarchy of our interests. For example, Hildebrandt (1875) found it remarkable that, "A family bereavement, which has moved us deeply and under whose immediate shadow we have fallen asleep late at night, is blotted out of our memory till with our first waking moment it returns to it again with disturbing violence. On the other hand, a wart on the forehead of a stranger whom we met in the street and to whom we gave no second thought after passing him *has* a part to play in our dream. . . ." Havelock Ellis (1899) also was aware that so far as the immediate past is concerned, it is mostly the trifling, the incidental, the "forgotten" impressions of daily life which reappear in our dreams.

Freud (1900) thought that this "most striking and least comprehensible characteristic of memory in dreams" can be made understandable by recalling that ". . . the sense of the dream . . . can only rightly be [judged] by its latent content. The irrelevant details from the day or days before the dreaming only supply material to the manifest dream; this function is the key to an understanding of their reappearance in the dream. . . . If we assume that the same need for transference on the part of repressed ideas which we have discovered in analysing the neuroses is also at work in dreams, two of the riddles of the dream are solved at a blow: the fact, namely, that every analysis of a dream shows some recent impression woven into its texture and that this recent element is often of the most trivial kind. . . . the reason why these recent and indifferent elements so frequently find their way into dreams as substitutes for the most ancient of all the dream-thoughts is that they have least to fear from the censorship imposed by resistance" (1900, 175, 563).

That is, the dream-forming processes prefer to take advantage of trivial and recent impressions in order to satisfy the demand of the repressed wish for material suitable for entering consciousness. Registered but not consciously perceived events may serve the infiltrating unconscious content like Trojan horses. This function of disguise is the reason that irrelevant impressions reappear in dreams.

This theory of transfer, or rather displacement, of psychic values demands five things: 1) The necessary cause of every dream is a repressed idea; 2) This repressed idea assimilates and strengthens the weak intensity of one or more indifferent and recent impressions, so that it or they enter into consciousness; 3) Indifferent and recent impressions are, so to say, free floating units. They are not yet tied to any well-defined associative realm, and thus the unconscious wishes, by absorbing them, may freely manipulate them; 4) These weak impressions are also useful in misleading the censorship as wishes pass from the first to the second psychical system; 5) Due to the union between the preconscious and unconscious thought, the indifferent impression as it is recalled in the dream will be distorted in many respects.

We have already seen that repressed wishes are not necessarily the cause of every dream. Let us turn, therefore, to the third of these five steps.

While agreeing with the observation that unattended-to impressions are indeed integrated into our psychic life in a manner different from that of the relevant ones, I shall suggest here an explanation implied by the consolidation theory of memory. The initiators of this theory, Muller and Pilzecker (1900), hypothesized the perseveration of some neural process as a prerequisite for stabilizing new learning. During this process, the not-yet-stabilized memory is vulnerable; new events may interfere with its structuralization, and cause retroactive inhibition. This theory gained new respectability through Hebb's influence (1949), who assumed reverberatory neural circuits which maintain the impression until the fixation of the memory traces have been completed. During the perseveration period, there is a degree of temporary inhibition of recall to protect, as it seems, the impression from possible interference. Walker (1958), and Walker and Tarte (1963) labelled this phenomenon "action decrement."

Now, the point is that peripheral, unattended-to impressions need a longer time for action decrement than do focalized experiences. Bryden (1971) found that not attended-to, in contrast to attended-to auditory material is better recalled when there is a delay in time before it can be assessed. The unattended-to impressions apparently must wait in line to be processed. Up to the end of this procedure, due to action decrement, they seem to be lost; only afterward are they able to reappear. This prolonged action decrement may explain a finding of Shevrin and Luborski (1958), who showed their subjects tachistoscopically exposed pictures. Subsequently, the subjects described and drew what they had seen as fully as possible. They were asked for a second full description and drawing immediately following the first recall, and again on the next day. On this occasion, they also told what they had dreamed the night before. Quite frequently, the authors say, items not noted in the first recall emerged in the second or third recalls. That is, we may assume that their belated emergence was caused by an action decrement; during their process of consolidation they were not available for recall.

Actually, Shevrin and Luborski's findings are scarcely surprising. A hundred years ago Helmholtz discovered the retrieval, in positive after images, of details not perceived consciously during the original observation. His finding was confirmed by Urbantschitsch (1907) in his experiments with eidetics. Potzl (1915) also described cases of delayed appearance in consciousness of stimuli not perceived at the moment of exposure. Exposing pictures tachistoscopically to a hallucinating patient with latent hemianopsia, Potzl observed the delayed emergence of some details in the hallucinations.

The crucial point, apparently, is the period of time during which one is concerned with the fate of the not attended-to stimuli. In immediate recall they seem to be represented rather poorly, and one gets the impression that they evaporated before getting established. Extending the range of observation to a day or so, one is led to the opposite conclusion, for then not attended-to stimuli appear rather tenacious.

We are not yet able to define precisely the time-table

of the processes involved in establishing long-term memory of the unattended-to inputs. At any rate, a few available evidences suggest that we are able to hold inputs in a temporary storage for a surprisingly long time, before they get fixed. For example, Fishbein, *et al.* (1971) deprived mice of REM sleep for two days immediately after one-trial training in an inhibitory avoidance task. Mice which received electroshock 5 minutes, 30 minutes, or one hour after the end of REM sleep deprivation displayed marked retention deficiencies. On the other hand, mice administered ECS 3, 6, or 12 hours after the termination of REM deprivation showed normal retention of learning.

This experiment demonstrates that the memory trace of a previous learning can be held in temporary storage, and thus be disrupted days after the original experience. In other words, we are able to hold input before consolidating it in longterm memory for a period measured in hours and not in seconds. While in temporary storage the input is not available, is "forgotten." Having become fixed, however, this input emerges spontaneously or at the demands of an appropriate situation.

The longer time needed to consolidate the unattended-to stimuli may, then, explain their reappearance in afterimages, in eidetic imagination, in subsequent recalls, in hallucinations, or in dreams. This consolidation, rather than the assumed motive of deceiving censorship, is its most likely explanation.

Does sleep contradict cognition?

Essential to Freud's theory is the idea that the dream is a disturbance of sleep, or rather, that dreams indicate a weakening of the intensity of sleep. Implied in this view is that sleep is, by definition, devoid of mental activity, and that the cognition necessary to construct a dream is made possible by a partial arousal. Sleep research supposedly supports this view: REM sleep is described as the period of dreaming, and significantly, during this stage of sleep signs of cortical arousal are identifiable.

In spite of its popularity, this idea does not hold up. To begin with, the EEG during sleep is indeed extremely fast and activated—but in cats, *not* in primates. In primates, the EEG more closely resembles the somewhat slowed and random pattern found in the initial transition from waking to sleep (Snyder, 1969). The popular stereotype of REM sleep—motor inhibition accompanied by activated EEG, the presumed evidence for cortical arousal—applies to cats only. The diagnosis of cortical arousal based on the evidence of a desynchronized EEG therefore appears to be questionable. It rests upon a blending of animal and human data that exaggerates the similarities and disregards the differences.

Furthermore, there are doubts about whether EEG activity in awareness and in sleep depicts the same mental functions. Johnson (1970) is of the opinion that the 8–12 Hz waves seen during waking, stage 1 sleep, REM sleep, hypnosis, and meditation do not come from the same generator. Ewarts (1962) found that in the cat different sets of neurons are active during waking and REM sleep, even though the EEG activity is similar; Johnson therefore wonders whether in man, as in other animals, there may be more than one source producing similar waves. If so, then similar EEG tracings may have different meanings; and until we are able to differentiate among them the contribution of EEG to the problem of arousal during sleep will remain in doubt.

The lack of a definitive answer to the above question is only a part of the story. The major point is that it is impossible to assume a similarity between mental activity during waking and REM sleep, based on EEG as the sole measurement. Johnson (1970) found that during wakefulness the threshold of arousal for the EEG, cardiovascular (HR), electrochemical (EDA), and finger pulse (FPR) are nearly the same, with significant EEG, EDA, and FPR responses occurring at the motor response threshold. HR changes were present, but were not quite significant. During sleep, however, nothing of this alliance of thresholds remained. The EEG response first appeared 30 decibels below that required for arousal and the motor response. The finger pulse response occurred 15 decibels below arousal threshold, and the heart rate response was clearly significant 5 decibels below arousal threshold. But the electrodermal response did not occur until there was EEG arousal and the motor response threshold was reached. This striking finding may demonstrate the proper way to define alertness psychophysiologically. EEG, EDA, and FPR in concert, as a syndrome, may define alertness; but not each measurement separately.

Fedio *et al.* (1961) are also of the opinion that EEG alone does not reliably identify states of consciousness. They found that schizophrenics, despite their having alpha block, failed to show behavioral arousal—that is, a reduced reaction time. Some schizophrenics even performed more slowly. Therefore, Fedio *et al.* suggest that separate and partially independent neural systems mediate the behavioral and the EEG arousal patterns.

We may sum up by saying that EEG indices as a sole measurement fail to identify mental activity during REM sleep. But in addition to giving up EEG as the proof and measurement of cortical arousal during REM sleep, we must also give up the premise that sleep is, by definition, devoid of mental activity.

In contradiction to earlier reports, it is now a well-established fact that subjects awakened from REM as well as NREM sleep report mental activity (Foulkes, 1962; Zimmerman, 1967). As Foulkes (1969) put it: "No point of absolute dream onset exists. . . . there is no point in the sleep cycle at which consciousness suddenly appears." Mental activity never ceases while we are alive, whether awake or asleep, tired or alert. It is, however, important to note that we generate two categories of mentation while asleep. The first is a rather dramatic, often bizarre and unreal story of the type we are used to calling a "dream"; the other is less elaborate and often expressly relates to our recent or forthcoming activities.

For a while, the REM periods of sleep were identified with the occurrence of "dreamy" mentation. The conviction that dreaming unfolds during the REM period was substantiated by correspondences found between measurable events during REM and temporal landmarks in the subsequent dream narratives. The rapid eye movements were regarded as scanning responses of the visual dream images.

However, Moskowitz and Berger (1969) have disproved this scanning hypothesis. According to their findings, in the great majority of cases the EEG pattern was totally inappropriate to the dream events. Since patterns, frequencies, velocities, and interval distributions of the REMs are constant in cat, monkey, and man, while visual imagery is highly variable from one REM period to another, clearly dreams and REMs are not synonymous. Such a conclusion is not surprising, since Goodenough *et al.* (1965) found as early as 1959 that in their dreamrecaller group a mean of 53 per cent of the awakenings during periods of ocular quiescence led to a recall of a dream. That is, visual imagery is possible without scanning movements of the eyes.

There is much more evidence available to support the statement that dreaming is not limited to REM periods. Zimmerman (1967) was able to demonstrate the occurrence of dreams during NREM sleep. "Deep" sleepers with high awakening thresholds reported dreams after 21 per cent of their NREM awakenings, whereas "light" sleepers with low awakening thresholds reported dreams after 71 per cent of their NREM awakenings. Similarly, Hobson *et al.* (1965) found that awakenings following transient periods of increased respiratory rate during NREM sleep are likely to yield dream reports. Foulkes and Vogel (1965) pointed out another aspect, that of sleep onset. This transitional state of consciousness generates an EEG pattern much like that during REM periods, but ordinarily without rapid eye movements. Yet, the hypnagogic imagery characteristic of this twilight state resembles regular dreams. And, finally, we also have experimental evidence that dreams are not confined to REM sleep.

Hersch *et al.* (1970) injected epinephrine, during stage 4 sleep, into 8 subjects. An equivalent amount of saline was injected the same night during another passage through stage 4. Subjects were awakened 10 minutes after each injection and asked to report on their cognitions. The stage of sleep did not change as a result of the injection; there was, however, an increase in the mean HR interbeat duration time in the 10 minute period after injection of epinephrine (but not after the injection of saline), and the dream reports were more vivid, more bizarre, more emotional, and more perceptual than conceptual as compared with those reported after the saline injection. The level of autonomic activity appears here as a precondition determining whether the ongoing cognition will be a dream or a thought. Their finding might be integrated with that of Hobson *et al.* (1965), to justify a new look at the conditions of dreaming.

Considering the evidence for dreaming during NREM sleep, we may regard the assigning of dreams to REM sleep as disproved. Dreams are scattered over all the hours of sleep, and occur during both REM and NREM sleep. Between dreams we also generate thoughtlike mentation, fairly well adapted to reality. It does not seem an exaggeration to say that we are cognizing continuously while we sleep. Therefore, the question to be answered by a theory of dreams is not how it happens that we are able to dream while sleeping, but rather how to explain the differences between these mentations.

Remember the microgenetic model of cognition and dynamic schemes. A dynamic scheme is unthinkable without an effort, a mental effort. The phenomenon of the tip-of-the-tongue shows the existence of active strategies of matching and mismatching in evolving ideas. However, during the different states of consciousness, there are differences in capacity to mobilize mental effort. While fatigued or drugged, one's mental effort is not sufficient to evolve the sought-for ideas from their schemes, and the product of cognition may be unusual or even bizarre as compared with controlled waking thoughts. In the opinion of Bergson (1901), the conditions prevailing during sleep are especially prone to produce cognition of low mental effort—that is to say, dreams.

While endorsing Bergson's general framework, I would

like to point to a correction necessitated by the discovery of two kinds of dreams. If we view these two kinds of dreams as products of a continuous mental activity, we must conclude that the waking thought-like mentation, usually assigned to NREM sleep, is generated in a relatively alert state; while stories more complicated in structure and not congruous with everyday experience (that is, the popular idea of dreams) are generated in a deeper sleep when one is less able to direct one's thinking. What mainly differentiates these two products is the degree of mental effort one is capable of mobilizing while they are processed.

This conclusion, which follows logically from accepting the product of cognition as a behavioral measurement of cerebral arousal, is well supported by an important experiment of Hernandez-Peon (1965). Hernandez-Peon thinks that the two major phases of sleep result from different degrees of inhibition directed by the same functional hypnogenic neuronal system against the vigilance system. The sleep system involves a number of pathways descending from the cortex through the limbic midbrain circuit, and also an ascending component coming up from the spinal cord through the medulla to the midbrain. Along the pathways of this circuit, stimulation with cholinergic substances elicits sleep. Hernandez-Peon was able to elicit deep (REM) sleep by injecting strong doses of acetylcholine, and light (NREM) sleep by weaker doses of the same chemostimulus.

The two phases of sleep only differ in the degree of inhibition of the vigilance system. This descending order of inhibition of the vigilance system from lesser (in NREM sleep) to deeper (in REM sleep) is, then, the neurophysiological substrate of the differences in the capacity to mobilize mental effort, and thus of generating two different kinds of dreams: a fringe type of waking thought, and a bizarre dream.

I am fully aware of the necessity to soften, so to speak, the edges of this picture. I have referred to REM and NREM periods as if they were clearcut phases of sleep unequivocally recognizable, physiologically as well as psychologically. In fact, however, there are indications that REM and NREM are not such clearly differentiated states of sleep as we used to think. To begin with, a distinction has been made between the tonic and phasic events of REM sleep (Moruzzi, 1963). The rapid eye movements, the concomitant muscular twitches, cardiovascular irregularities, respiratory changes, and fluctuations in penile tumescence are phasic; they occur only intermittently during REM sleep. The activated EEG, together with the motor inhibition, are long lasting and continuous throughout the same period—that is, they are tonic. Recently, Pivik and Dement (1970) described a phasic suppression of the tonic EMG during NREM sleep in human subjects. In view of phasic events during NREM sleep, the distinction between REM and NREM sleep appears to be a first, global approach to a rather complex phenomenon.

Dreamy mentation, then, is not confined to REM sleep. Rather it is the concomitant—and also a measure—of a phasic inhibition of the vigilance system. It is therefore suggested here that we view the dream as a cognition processed at a stage of deep inhibition of vigilance, the precise timetable of which is not yet known, except that it is prevalent from time to time during REM as well as during NREM sleep.

It is now important to emphasize that the differences between the two kinds of dreams are not determined by

properties of sleep. For example, Fiss, *et al.* (1966) awakened their subjects from an REM period, and from stage
2 or 3 sleep. Immediately after awakening, they handed
the subject a TAT card, asking him to make up a story
about it. Stories produced after interrupted REM sleep
were longer, more complex, visual, bizarre, emotional,
and vivid than stories told during control waking periods.
That is, the level of cognition characteristic of the particular sleep stage was carried over into the waking state.
Similarly, Destrooper and Broughton (1969) reported that
after a NREM awakening just before the expected fourth
REM period, subjects' speech on two occasions suddenly
shifted to an unrelated topic during coherent reports of
earlier dreams.

These observations indicate that vigilance waxes and
wanes according to a circadian rhythm. Each level of vigilance is characterized by a different degree of capacity to
mobilize mental effort. The degree of mental effort is
responsible for the level of cognition, that is, whether one
is able to go through all the steps of microgenesis or will
stop prematurely at one of the preparatory phases. The
dream bears the stamp of a deep inhibition of the vigilance system; the cognition of NREM sleep, on the other
hand, evidences a lesser inhibition of this system and
therefore a microgensis pushed to the fringe of waking
controlled thought. In a word, we propose to explain the
existence and the characteristics of dreams by a continuum of mental effort, rather than by a continuum of
defenses against instinctual drives.

Paradoxically, this explanatory change need not effect
the clinical use of dreams. Dreams are enigmatic and
their meaning is ambiguous at best. Whether one prefers
to decipher them by using free association a la Freud, or

amplification a la Jung, the basic fact is that dreams are interpreted rather than translated from one language to another. The meaning of a dream is always an amalgam of the biographical context of the dreamer and of the frame of view of the interpreter. For example, Alexander the Great is said to have once seen in a dream a satyr *(satyros)* dancing on his shield. Since the dream happened to occur when Alexander was besieging Tyros, Aristander interpreted it as *sa Tyros,* that is, Tyros is thine. Encouraged, Alexander went on to conquer Tyros.

Had Alexander dreamed this same dream while entertaining himself in his palace, I am sure that Aristander would have suggested another interpretation, neither less pleasant nor plausible. A Freudian interpreter might sense the sexual connotation of a satyr, and stop the stream of association at an appropriate place. A Jungian might see in it a reflection of the animal aspects of human existence, and amplify it without seeking further proof. A microgenetic interpreter might wonder whether the worried dreamer was trying to think out something concerning Tyros, but was unable to evolve it fully from its dynamic scheme and so stopped prematurely at one of its preparatory phases, that of the *satyros.* Each of these interpretations is as possible and as arbitrary as the others.

If, however, instead of interpreting dreams we use them for demonstrating a general theory of behavior, then the conception of a continuum of defenses and the metastructure built upon it must be given up. This continuum demands a stepwise relaxation of defenses from controlled waking thought through daydreams and fringe-type waking thought to dreams. Parallel to this descending order of defenses, repressed wishes should be recognizable in an ascending order up to their fullest expression in dreams; but as we have seen, the actualization of instinctual drives is far less possible in dreams than in daydreams and early memories.

On the other hand, the microgenetic approach does not postulate the incessant urge of repressed wishes as the necessary cause of dreaming. Instead this approach emphasizes the fact of ongoing cognition: the living brain never ceases to process information. Cognition is ongoing, but its adaptedness to reality is variable. Cognition has as many levels as has consciousness. In fact, the level of cognition is one of the distinctive features of the level of consciousness. They are different aspects of a common essence.

Wakefulness is a graded phenomenon. The continuum runs from facing the world openly, through a selective awareness of special stimuli, to the phasic contact called fatigue or drowsiness. All of these levels of wakefulness have a characteristic interaction with the environment. The fully awake person, due to his momentary extraversion, is ready to discover the world and cope with it adaptively. In daydreams, he never seeks outer stimuli, but is momentarily introverted; received messages are assimilated into the ongoing mental processes. A fatigued or drowsy man struggles to maintain contact with his surroundings, but he is able to do so only phasically. In full sleep, he recedes from all activity that relates to the world. This passivity is the main behavioral characteristic of sleep. But cognition does not cease even in the midst of passivity. We get reports on mental activity from REM as well as from NREM sleep; it is only their level of organization that shifts. These many levels of cognition demonstrate that the capacity to mobilize mental effort for evolving cognition through its phases of microgenesis fluctuates according to a circadian rhythm. Dreams are generated while one is capable of only low mental effort.

Chapter Five

Schizophrenia—An Information-Processing Theory

Intuition without verification?

WHAT IS SCHIZOPHRENIA? An answer is usually not given promptly, and there is a good chance that any answer will not be accepted unanimously. Indeed, Cancro (1970) doubts whether a review of research directions in schizophrenia is possible at all. "Of what relevance is it to review directions in an area in which there are virtually no stable coordinates?" he exclaims. "It is almost as meaningless as speaking of north and south in intergalactic space."

The most convenient way to approach schizophrenia might be to appeal to the father of the concept, E. Bleuler. Unfortunately, we do not even agree about what precisely Bleuler said. For example, Meehl (1962) suggests that thought disorder is what rings the diagnostic bell. A patient may experience intense ambivalence, conscious hatred of family figures, and be pananxious and withdrawn, all of which may indicate schizophrenia; but if the patient adds, "Naturally, I am growing my father's hair," this last statement will weigh more heavily than all the other symptoms together. In this respect, concludes Meehl, we are still Bleulerians.

Could E. Bleuler agree with this? If we accept his son as the authoritative interpreter of his thought, the answer will be no, he could not. For M. Bleuler (1968) emphasizes that "The schizophrenic psychosis can be characterized neither by the final loss of any function nor by the production of any new morbid process. It must be characterized by a loss of equilibrium of two different, in themselves normal ways of living." Indeed, Ellen West (Binswanger, 1961) was diagnosed by E. Bleuler as schizophrenic in spite of the absence of any thought disturbance. Her case might be considered by Janet as a paradigm of the pathological consequence of an *idée fixe*, but Bleuler as well as Binswanger were sure that what she suffered from was schizophrenia. Apparently E. Bleuler thought that autism —the over-valence of inner life over the consensual reality—is pathognomic enough to allow the diagnosis of schizophrenia.

It is only fair to add that Kraepelin, also consulted by the family of Ellen West, was of the opinion that she had a manic-depressive psychosis. Making a decision between such opposing views would demand a clear definition of the concept of schizophrenia, and, of course, a diagnosis dependent on this definition. Surprisingly enough, we do not have any such definition. Moreover, Langfeldt (1969) thinks that E. Bleuler's description of schizophrenia is mainly responsible for the prevailing confusion in clinical practice. E. Bleuler included, in the group of schizophrenias, typical melancholias and manias, most hallucinatory confusions, Wernicke's disease, almost all cases of hypochondriasis with poor prognosis, and many more pathological phenomena. This is too much to be covered by one definition. As a remedy, Langfeldt suggests differentiating between genuine schizophrenia and schizophreniform psychoses. He describes genuine types of schizophrenia as characterized by a significant break in personality, emotional blunting, catatonic stupor, and restlessness, as well as the symptoms of depersonalization and derealization. "All psychoses which—because they involve hallucinations and delusions—may have a superficial similarity with the genuine schizophrenias but are lacking the essential symptoms of these, should be diagnosed as schizophreniform psychoses."

This is not a definition of schizophrenia. Nevertheless, if we adhere strictly to a minimum of symptomatology as the *sine qua non* of diagnosis, it may improve the present situation. At present, as Cancro (1970) observed, a patient may be diagnosed as schizophrenic by one psychiatrist, and as manic-depressive by another, the only difference in the circumstances being that he has changed institutions. This situation could be considerably ameliorated if psychiatrists would agree to consistently apply certain criteria in diagnosing schizophrenia. Alas, psychiatrists often allow themselves, instead, to be deceived by self-assurances, telling themselves that it is more difficult to describe schizophrenia than to recognize it, and that the experienced psychiatrist feels it intuitively. However, intuition should be subject to subsequent scrutiny and proof. Diagnosis, after all, is testable. And since psychiatric illnesses are not referred to pathologists for examination, psychiatrists should be careful in applying certain criteria in diagnosing schizophrenia.

M. Bleuler (1968) used to make the diagnosis of schizophrenia only if at least three of the following symptoms were present: 1) thought disturbances; 2) a change of emotional life; 3) catatonic symptoms; 4) delusions or hallucinations. Meehl (1962) cites the symptoms of thought disorder, interpersonal aversiveness, anhedonia, and ambivalence. Whether a psychiatrist accepts M. Bleuler's, Langfeldt's, Meehl's, or some other authority's criteria, he should apply them consistently. Doing so would not restrain his freedom of intuition; it would only require that he look for evidence in accord with a basic symptomatology. Only when psychiatrists diagnose on such a basis will we be able to reliably study the psychodynamics and therapeutics of schizophrenia.

The symptomatology of early schizophrenia

As far as the psychopathology of schizophrenia is concerned, current interest is directed almost exclusively to early schizophrenia. Psychopathological research reflects here, rather closely, the changing world of clinical psychiatry. Summing up his lifetime experience, M. Bleuler (1968) was able to demonstrate that catastrophic schizophrenia—acute onset followed immediately by chronic severe psychosis—which was often seen at the beginning of this century is now practically dying out. Furthermore, the proportion between most severe and milder chronic psychoses has changed. The milder chronic conditions have increased, while the severe chronic conditions have decreased as a result of improved therapy. The real improvement, so argues Bleuler, has not much to do with the changes in somatic therapies, but rather with the fact that patients are no longer mishandled, that isolation in isolation rooms and failure to discharge patients at the right moment no longer occur. In other words, we are now aware that chronic schizophrenia is contaminated by the conditions of prolonged hospitalization, and that a reliable analysis of schizophrenia must be based on its early stages.

Recently, McGhie and Chapman (1961) considered the psychopathology of early schizophrenia. They do not clarify the criteria they applied in arriving at their diagnoses, and they mention only that the subsequent course of the illness confirmed the original diagnosis. But it is clear that their research dealt with nonparanoid early schizophrenics. Their patients were encouraged to be introspective, and to describe their experiences as fully as possible. The authors then analyzed the self-reports according to changes in attention, perception, motility, thinking, and affects.

For example, the patients complain of not being able to focus their attention. "It's as if I am too wide awake—very, very alert. I can't relax at all. Everything seems to go through me. I just can't shut things out," says one; and another reports, "Everything seems to grip my attention although I am not particularly interested in anything. I am speaking to you just now but I can hear noises going on next door and in the corridor. I find it difficult to shut these out and it makes it more difficult for me to concentrate on what I am saying to you. Often the silliest things that are going on seem to interest me. That's not even true; they don't interest me, but I find myself attending to them and wasting a lot of time this way. I know that sounds like laziness but it's not really."

The physical qualities of the world are intensified to the patient. Everything is louder and noisier, colors are more vivid than usual. McDonald (1960) reports that a patient of his described it this way: "What I do want to explain, if I can, is the exaggerated state of awareness in which I lived before, during, and after my acute illness. . . . By the time I was admitted to the hospital I reached a stage of 'wakefulness' when the brilliance of light on a window sill or the color of blue in the sky would be so important it would make me cry. . . ."

McGhie and Chapman describe their patients' difficulty in understanding speech as disturbances in the process of perception, but that seems to be a mistake. The elaboration of meaning is clearly a function that is different from, let us say, registering colors. For example, one of their patients explained: "When people are talking the words are going on and on and I don't understand them. It's extremely confusing—like going into a blank wall." Such a disturbance belongs in a category of its own: a failure to integrate and arrive at the meaning of the processed information.

Further, there are changes in motility and bodily awareness. "I am not sure of my own movements any more. It's very hard to describe this . . . I found recently that I was thinking of myself doing things before I would do them. If I am going to sit down, for example, I have got to think of myself and almost see myself sitting down before I do it. . . . All this makes me move much slower. I take more time to do things because I am always conscious of what I am doing. If I could just stop noticing what I am doing, I would get things done a lot faster." The patient is slowed down; he becomes aware, not of his body as defined by McGhie and Chapman, but rather of his actions. Automatic actions, like sitting, eating, dressing, are now performed in an anxiously planned manner; they are deautomatized.

The well-known thought disturbances may be exemplified, though not fully described, by this striking piece of introspection: "When I am trying to think of something I am like a railway engine running along a line where someone keeps changing the points."

Such experiences may end up in a loss of the sense of control, and a growing alienation from the patient's own thoughts and feelings. "Things just happen to me now and I have no control over them," said one. "I don't seem to have the same say in things any more. At times I can't even control what I want to think about. I am starting to feel pretty numb about everything because I am becoming an object and objects don't have feelings."

Thus, following McGhie and Chapman's description, except for a few changes, we may point out six major phenomena of early schizophrenia: 1) An inability to focus attention; 2) Hyperaesthesia; 3) An inability to integrate and arrive at the meaning of the processed information; 4) Deautomatization; 5) Thought disturbances; and 6) A loss of self-determination.

McGhie and Chapman summarize their study by stating that the earliest reported symptoms of schizophrenia indicate that a decrease of the "selective and inhibitory functions of attention" is the primary disorder. Their argument is not unfamiliar; however, this interpretation is not able to suggest a unified theory of the symptomatology of early schizophrenia. To begin with, hyperaesthesia is hardly understandable as the outcome of a defective attentiveness. In fact, it seems to evidence a peak in selectiveness rather than a defect in it. And then, deautomatization, that is, the meticulous planning of simple, overskilled actions, can not be explained by a decrease in the capacity to select and eliminate. Something else must be compelling enough to cause the patient to think out his movements before making them.

The symptoms enumerated above range from information encoding to its decoding. There is a rather fair consensus today that "on logical, phenomenological, and empirical grounds," as Neisser (1967) put it, we have to assign to verbal coding the main responsibility for conserving information. Therefore, if we hope to reduce the symptomatology of early schizophrenia to a single core phenomenon, we must follow up the vicissitudes of the auditory-verbal modality in information processing.

The auditory-verbal modality in information processing

The beginnings of representational thinking in humans are to be found, according to Piaget (1947), at the sixth phase of sensorimotor intelligence, that is, from 18 months on. Piaget cites two pieces of evidence: firstly, at this age the child becomes capable of delayed imitation, that is, producing a copy after the model has disappeared; and secondly, the child simultaneously arrives at the simplest form of symbolic play, for example, he pretends to sleep for fun, while he is actually wide awake. How does it happen that the child is suddenly able to represent events in the absence of ongoing sensory information? It happens because the child has become able to use a new means for holding his memories: language. Words are the wings which raise and hold him above the immediacy of sense data. The appearance of language is the most salient event in the stream of childhood. Actually, it effects a caesura in the life-history; everything that happens in the preverbal period may be regarded as prehistory, detached, far-off, and in a sense, incomprehensible.

Obviously, early childhood is the period of human life which is richest in experience. Everything is new to the newborn child. "No Columbus, no Marco Polo has ever seen stranger and more fascinating and thoroughly absorbing sights than the child who learns to perceive, to taste, to smell, to touch, to hear and to use his body, his senses, and his mind. No wonder that the child shows an insatiable curiosity. He has the whole world to discover" (Schachtel, 1947). The child does indeed manage to discover the world, its sights and smells, its gratifications and sufferings; but, astonishingly, he will have no memories of all those exciting first experiences, perplexities and victories. The period richest in experience is the poorest in remembrance. Freud's opinion was that the Edipal conflict, leading to repression, is responsible for this amnesia; the repression of infantile sexuality leads progressively to the forgetting of infantile experiences in general. Schachtel points out that even the most profound and prolonged psychoanalysis does not lead to a recovery of childhood memory. I would like to add, especially not to a recovery of preverbal memories. "Childhood amnesia, then, may be due to a formation of the memory functions which make them unsuitable to accommodate childhood experience, rather than exclusively to a center repressing objectionable material which, without such repression, could and would be remembered." Schachtel suggests that experience increasingly assumes the form of conventional cliches, and therefore the categories or schemata of adult memory cannot preserve the idiosyncratic experiences of early childhood.

I fully agree with Schachtel that infantile amnesia is a result of the structural properties of memory functions. However, I disagree with his emphasis on conventional cliches, and instead, I would like to point to the role of words in conserving our experiences. Words, said Bergson, are the carriers of memory. The most striking proofs of this are supplied by experiments which display the process of encoding visually received information. Sperling (1970) requested his subjects to write down letters presented to them tachistoscopically. This simple experiment yielded much evidence to support the centrality of verbal encoding. First, all his subjects said they rehearsed the letters subvocally. Then, subjects did not begin to write until a second or more after the exposure. But, since short-term visual information normally fades rapidly, usually within about one-fourth of a second, auditory rehearsal is the only logical alternative explanation. This is also why I suggest that implicit verbalization is the only possible explanation for the appearance of delayed imitation in the second year of life.

The most important evidence of Sperling is the measurement of AS (auditory similarity) deficits. An AS deficit is defined as the relative decrement in performance—that is, errors in recognition—caused by replacing a stimulus composed of acoustically different letters (for example, F,H,Q, and Y) with acoustically similar letters (for example, B, C, D, and G). The main finding of this experiment was that in the usual test of visual recall, deficits caused by visual similarity are small, whereas AS deficits are large. That auditory similarity should be a significant factor even in a task that involves only looking at letters and writing them down, with never any overt auditory representation, is prima facie evidence of a role for auditory memory in visual recall tasks.

A further evidence of the role of auditory modality in information processing comes from research on aphasia.

Luria (1966) describes a patient who had suffered a motor aphasia. While his tongue was clamped between his teeth (for the purposes of the experiment), he was able to understand descriptive sentences, such as; "Today there was a dense fog and driving was extremely difficult." As he said later: "I understood right away. I pictured to myself how hard it was to drive in the fog."

On the other hand, it took the patient a while to grasp the meaning of a sentence of this sort: "Place the comb to the left of the pencil." To master the same sentence, however, while his tongue was between his teeth, required 12 times longer than he had needed before. He solved it by trial and error. As he put it: "I figured it out with my hand, that's how I did it." When he was given the sentence, "The girl is bigger than the boy," and was asked, with his tongue compressed, which of the two is smaller, he was totally lost. The patient spent minutes tracing the few words with his finger, to no avail. Later, he explained, "I can read it and it seems I understand it, but somehow I just can't figure it out." Once his tongue was freed, he solved the same problem in ten seconds, saying: "The girl is bigger . . . the girl is bigger. That means the boy is smaller." Then, he added spontaneously: "I can picture it in my mind, but, you see, it just doesn't work. I can't get it. But if I say it out loud, I understand. Then I can figure it out right away. I don't understand what it is that helps, but when my tongue is held tight it seems as if the words are being held back and I can't link them up."

We see here a linear development. With every additional step of complexity, the role of the auditory component in thinking became more and more apparent. It is not clear what it is that disrupts the subvocal rehearsal in motor aphasics, thus making them dependent on outside sounds. Perhaps they disrupt the conversion of the subvocal rehearsal into auditory representation, and substitute the hearing of words from outside. At any rate, one must agree with Sokolov's (1969) dictum that, "There is no aphasia without disruptions of internal speech." These experiments, which are supported by many related studies also available in the literature, make it apparent that while encoding and decoding are processed by an interrelated activation of modalities, in hearing people from the age of five (Conrad, 1971), the auditory-verbal one has the lead.

This conclusion applies also to what is measured by reaction time. Mental processes do not yield easily to quantification; since, however, their actualization takes time, the reaction time (RT) has become one of the most important measurable dimensions of mental processes. It is now well established that in normal persons auditory reaction time is faster than visual (Teichner, 1954). The primacy of the auditory modality is further underlined by the intriguing effects that auditory stimuli delivered after a visual stimulus have on the visual. Confirming earlier findings, Nickerson (1970) reports that an auditory stimulus may facilitate the response to a visual stimulus even when the sound *follows* the light (provided the interval is up to 120 msec.). Reaction time to a light stimulus alone is significantly longer.

Apparently, we may assign an exceptional position to the auditory modality in normals. Concerning schizophrenia, Venables and O'Connor (1959) reported that intact paranoid schizophrenics, like normal subjects, have faster reactions to auditory than to visual stimuli. On the other hand, all nonparanoid patients and withdrawn paranoid patients show slower reaction to auditory than to visual stimuli. Significantly, Sutton, and Zubin (1961) have shown that reactions to light stimuli do not yield differences between patients and normals. In their reaction to sound stimuli, however, schizophrenics have a disproportionately longer retardation than normals. Furthermore, Gamburg (1965) has found schizophrenic patients to be impaired in both the motor and autonomic components of the orienting reflex to sound only.

In light of these findings, it will be, I presume, reasonable to take the loss of dominance of auditory modality as our starting point. Actually, Callaway (1969) has already considered this possibility. "Certainly, there is something odd about the auditory channel in schizophrenics. Does the schizophrenic have some difficulty with auditory information because of his disordered monitor plans, or are his plans disordered because of some defect in his handling of auditory data? This would seem to be a fruitful area for investigation." This is what I shall attempt here —to show that the possible antecedent of the symptomatology of early schizophrenia is a disturbance in the auditory-verbal modality in information processing.

The delay in the auditory-verbal modality, and the symptomatology of early schizophrenia

Unlike other productions of the schizophrenic syndrome, let us say thought disturbances or catatonic rigidity, deautomatization usually attracts very little analytical attention. It is surprising enough because patients express themselves in this respect very clearly. One of McGhie and Chapman's patients said, "I have to do everything step by step, nothing is automatic now. Everything has to be considered." Another patient agreed. "People just do things but I have to watch first to see how you do things. I have to think out most things first and know how to do them before I do them." These complaints hint at a disturbance of behavior control.

Control is, indeed, an essential ingredient of all information systems. Our output performances are accompanied by devices of control which feed back to a center the information about the results of the actions done so far.

Among the many contributions to this field, I would like to draw special attention to a seminal idea of Holst (1950, 1954). He has ingeniously adduced a variety of data supporting the conception that much of the organization of behaviour is attributable to a matching process by which feedback from action is compared with "efference copies." For example, the movement of the retinal image and the nerve impulses traveling from the eye to the brain are the same while scanning a stable environment or while looking straight at an external motion. Nevertheless, we are able to make a distinction as to the source of the movement. That is only understandable, suggests Holst, by hypothesizing an "efference copy." A command from a higher center causes a specific activation in a lower center, which gives rise to a specific efference to the effector, that is, to a muscle, a joint, or even the whole organism. This central stimulus situation is what he calls "efference copy."

The existence and the effect of such an efference copy becomes apparent if the effectors happen to be immobilized. If a subject's eye is fixed and the muscle receptors narcotized, then his wanting to turn his eye to the right will produce an appropriate efference copy, but it will not be matched by any reafference due to the paralysis of the eye muscles. The subject will report that the surroundings have jumped to the right. Every intended but unfulfilled eye movement results in the illusion of a quantitative movement of the surroundings in the same direction. Since nothing happens here on the afferent pathways, this false perception can only result from the activity originated by the intention to move the eye.

Also, by reversing the situation, that is, supplying reafference by turning the paralyzed eye mechanically to the right in the absence of intention (and also of efference copy) to do it, the subject will report that the surroundings move to the left.

That is, proprioception of scanning of a stable environment presupposes an integration of efference copy and related reafference. With efference copy alone, or reafference alone, the subject will attribute the movement to his surroundings. The direction of this attributed movement is a function of the pattern of failing congruency: an intention not followed by reafference leads to a movement of the same direction projected in the environment, while afferentation not preceded by intention causes the perception of an environmental motion opposite to the direction of the eye movement.

There is much more evidence to support the thesis of efference copy produced by an intention. For example, in a series of experiments on human position sense, Merton (1964) reports that when the joint and the skin of the thumb are anaesthesized without any effect on the muscles, after an hour or so the subject becomes quite insensitive to passive movements of the joints of whatever range or rapidity. If an intended movement is restrained by holding the thumb, the subject nevertheless believes he has moved it. These illusions of movement are only understandable as the conscious registration of an efference copy produced by an intention. The pattern of sequential actualization of behaviour initiated by the subject is thus as follows: (1) intention; (2) efference copy; (3) a matching process, that is, comparing the feedback information with the efference copy; (4) holding the complex of excitation until a congruency is achieved, either by attributing the performance to ourselves or projecting it on the environment; and (5) then inhibiting it. Here inhibition is a result of congruency between two ideas, so to speak, while in the context of psychodynamics, inhibition would arise out of the incompatibility between drives and defences.

I would like to suggest that the schizophrenic patients who suffer from deautomatization stand at the midpoint between the two extremes of performance without experiencing the efference copy, and experiencing the efference copy without performance. The schizophrenic patient performs his intentions, albeit slowly. And so it happens that he has a double experience: because of the delay in matching by feedback, he becomes aware of his own efference copy, and this awareness slows the execution of his intention. Since information is verbally encoded, it is only logical to assume that the efference copies are also verbal programs. Luria's experiment on aphasia demonstrates that rather clearly. The retarded auditory reaction time, characteristic of schizophrenic patients, is evidence of a delay in the matching of behavior sequences with their central representations. Such a delay in reafference, then, is the reason that schizophrenic patients become aware of their efference copies of which the normal subject is not aware, because of the prompt and automatic actualization of his intention.

The patient's failure to arrive at the meaning of the processed information can also be explained according to our frame of reference. Beginning with Osgood *et al.* (1957), a small group of researchers have succeeded in establishing the view that "perceiving" a word consists of encoding it within a number of different aspects or attributes. Wickens (1970) was able to show that, while encoding, we are particularly sensitive to the semantic attributes of the words, mildly reactive to the method of their physical presentation—for instance, number of syllables and phonemes—and essentially impervious to their syntactical characteristics. Thus, the meaning of a word, seen or heard, is an integration of a bundle of attributes; it is a vector whose value is determined by a number of components.

The view that words are encoded on a number of dimensions, and that their meaning is only achieved after the entries along these dimensions have been made makes the time factor important. The attributes of a word are not considered simultaneously; its meaning, as a sequentially actualized integration, accumulates across time. Although the process of encoding is performed "with tremendous alacrity and proficiency" as Wickens put it, nevertheless, it takes time. If one has not enough time for the processing, as in experiments on subception, the meaning of the word will not be fully evolved. Since the word in these experiments is presented very briefly, and the subject is not able to encode it along its pertinent dimensions, the meaning of the perceived word thus will reflect its fragmentary encoding. In other situations, a disturbance of the smooth flow of encoding through its successive states may result in intrusion errors, that is, in productions which are errors if compared with the final meaning of the sought-for word, but which match fairly well some of the semantic, sensory, or other attributes of this word.

It follows, then, that in order to communicate with our fellow humans, the processing of meaning must be fluent and rapid. The process of encoding symbols into these multiple dimensions is done "with deftness and automaticity associated only with a highly practiced skill. Thus it is, and only thus, that we are able to understand the rapid and variegated flow of conversation" (Wickens, 1970). That is why the schizophrenic patient is doomed to failure in his struggle to understand the meaning conveyed to him; his auditory reaction time is retarded as compared with that of normals. This delay disturbs the full evolution of the meaning of individual words, and consequently the required integration of words into a meaningful message. The patients of McGhie and Chapman (1961) described this situation rather clearly. One of them said, "When people are talking the words are going on and on and I don't understand them. It's extremely confusing—like going into a blank wall." Another patient reported, "I am slow in everything and everything is too quick. People speak to me but they go too quick for me to pick up."

In a study of experimentally-induced delay of auditory feedback, Lee (1951) has shown that any failure in the feedback will lead to a repetition of the signal word. Indeed, it is a common observation that schizophrenic patients responding in Word Association Test often repeat the signal word. This echolalia, which is presumably caused by a slowed down auditory-verbal processing, may end up in "semantic satiation" (Amster, 1964), that is, in a further loss of relevance and meaning due to a recurrent echoing. The schizophrenic patient thus encounters more than one difficulty in his attempt to understand what is being said.

The thought disturbances of schizophrenics have been evaluated in two opposing ways. "It looks," said E. Bleuler (1911), "as though ideas of a certain category . . . were thrown into one pot, mixed, and subsequently picked out at random. . . ." Cameron (1938), on the other hand, was able to show that even when dealing with hypothetical and very abstract matters in problems imposed from without, schizophrenic patients show for the most part a tendency to stick to the subject. "While their attempts do not satisfactorily dispose of the problem, their content hovers around it. . . . There seems to be . . . a fundamental disorder of concept-formation, in which the function may be considered either as arrested at an intermediate stage before it can be completed, or as reduced through disintegration to a simpler level of prelogical reasoning."

This dilemma posed by Cameron has unfortunately been disregarded by researchers as well as by clinicians. Most of us prefer a theory of regression, either in psychoanalytical terms or in terms of the concrete-abstract hypothesis. In fact, however, neither of these variants succeed in substantiating their claims to explain what happens. According to Freud (1911), schizophrenia is a "narcissistic neurosis," an outcome of an intrapsychic conflict, like hysteria. What differentiates neuroses is their level of regression, and schizophrenia represents the deepest regression. Even if it could be proved that schizophrenic symptoms are defensive activities purposefully related to unconscious conflicts over interpersonal relations, the peculiarities of schizophrenic language and thinking will demand a separate explanation. If we let the patient regress to a preverbal, primary narcissistic experience, what hope can we have of explaining idiosyncratic verbal productions? Besides, Cameron (1938) was able to show that the causal reasoning of schizophrenic patients does evidence many signs of change, but none of regression.

Another influential variant of the concept of regression is the concrete-abstract hypothesis. Benjamin and Watt (1968) pointed out that the assumed shift to the use of more concrete words is, according to Chapman (1964), coincidental with meaning strength. However, the preference for the stronger or more commonly used meaning is explained by inattention to contextual cues, and not by a shift or regression to less evolved modes of thinking. The dilemma posed by Cameron remains—whether the fundamental thought disturbance in schizophrenia may be considered as an arrest at an intermediate stage, or a reduction caused by disintegration and regression.

Among the categories of thought disturbances elaborated by Cameron, the loose, asyndetic clusters replacing well-defined concepts may be regarded as the most important. The consequence of this disturbance is that the schizophrenic attributes a false equivalence to several terms which in the normal might belong to the fringe of a conceptual structure. It is this use of approximation metonyms, Cameron observed, that lends to schizophrenic language a great deal of its peculiar flavor of elusiveness. These overinclusions raise two questions. First, why is the schizophrenic unable to eliminate these related but irrelevant sidetracks and produce coherent structures, instead of his characteristic vague, asyndetic clusters? Second, how can we explain the origin of these productions?

Since the beginning of this century a few researchers have suggested that thought disturbances only make apparent the usual way of evolving ideas and words. In his study on the flight of ideas, Aschaffenburg (1902) pointed out that a compulsion to verbalize all thought differentiates the speech of the hypomanic from that of the normal. Clang associations come to the mind of the normal as well, but he denies them verbalization. It is not the production of clang associations which is pathological, but rather the compulsion to verbalize them, that is, the inability to restrict the dynamic scheme (usually labelled the anticipatory scheme) to what is relevant for the moment.

The most outspoken among these authors was Schilder (1920). Analyzing evidence available in the literature, he concluded that, "It is a recognized fact that images and thoughts pass through various (preparatory, transitional) stages before they appear in a clear (conscious) form." The evolving of a thought, however, can be interrupted before its completion by even a minor interference. For example, Stransky (1905) instructed normal subjects to relax and verbalize all their associations to a stimulus word. He found perseverations, fusions of words (contamination), associations of contrast, and clang associations. "According to the analysis presented here," Schilder said, "these formations are also preparatory steps, that is, developmental phases of normal thought."

In other words, concepts as well as percepts are not immediately available in their complete form. At first, we have a scheme (or "sphere" as Schilder referred to it, borrowing a term from Kulpe) of the sought for. This scheme contains associative as well as meaningfully related contents. Clang associations, perseverations, contaminations, and symbols are steps in the evolving of a concept. Relaxation, distraction, or pathology may disturb this process; the result will then be a superficial association, a contaminated thought, or a symbol-like expression, instead of the exact word sought for.

The microgenesis of percepts, delineated by Sander (1928), and the experiments on the successive encoding of the many attributes of a word (Bower, 1967; Wickens, 1970) may be regarded as major events in establishing the Aschaffenburg-Schilder approach to thought disturbances. These experiments, however, only depict the registering and elaboration of information originating in the environment. To complete the picture, we are in need of a parallel theory concerning thought and speech generation. And indeed we have one—the theory of memory codes.

Considering the striking discrepancy between the very limited number of pieces of informations one can hold in immediate memory, and the virtually limitless amount of information stored in longterm memory, G. Miller (1956) suggested that the only way we are able to store so much information is by "chunking" it into units, or codes. It is possible that a code set is recoded into a higher code order, and that eventually this whole sequence is represented in memory by a single code. Thus, in order to recall any of the information within the chunk, we must necessarily first receive the code containing this information. An associative view seems to imply a representation in memory of the stimulus, a representation of the response, and finally a representation of the association between them. The coding view, on the other hand, assumes that there is only one representation in memory, the code, which includes a number of separate pieces of information.

Once recovered, all the information represented in the code is available for recall (Johnson, 1970, 1972). This, I

think, explains the overinclusions and metonymic approx-
imations of schizophrenic patients. Generating speech, all
of us begin by recovering memory codes. These codes,
however, are not readymade clumps of information. One
has to actively select the specified one, and eliminate the
others which are related to, but not pertinent to, the
requirements of the moment. Normal subjects usually
succeed, while schizophrenics fail attempting this performance. Schizophrenics fail in progressing from the
code to the specified information; nevertheless, their production is "by no means sheer nonsense as may at first
glance have appeared to be the case" (Cameron, 1938).
Certainly—since their production, however loose and
overinclusive, is still related to their intention.

The genesis of schizophrenic disturbances of thought
and speech may be regarded then as explained by this
convincing convergence of clinical observation and experimental evidences. As to the other question posed
above, why the schizophrenic is not able to eliminate
related but momentarily not relevant side tracks, we have
already seen that even slight disturbances may influence
the process of evolving from the scheme (code) to the
required information. And as far as schizophrenic disturbance is concerned, I would like to stress again their retarded auditory reaction time. We have already considered the possibility that this retardation badly effects their
internal speech (the existence of which was inferred,
among other things, from Luria's experiment on aphasia).
This very disturbance, which may cause deautomatization, is also mainly responsible for the schizophrenic's
difficulty in accomplishing the process of decoding.

If we view an internal interference due to a retarded
auditory reaction time as the basic disorder of schizophre-

nia, we have to be aware of the emotional concomitant of such an impediment. The schizophrenic's inability to think in a directed manner may engender the feeling of having lost self-determination. This loss of sense of autonomy, which begins with a gap between the dynamic scheme and the experienced result, may end up in a split; the me-ness of the experiences may fade away, and be replaced by a quality of threatening alienation.

A few researchers prefer another aspect of information processing. Weckowicz and Blewett (1959) suggest that the abnormalities of thinking and perception are secondary, and causally related to a basic inability to control the direction of attention. McGhie and Chapman (1961) endorsed this suggestion, because their clinical findings seem to point in the same direction; accordingly, they think that "if schizophrenia is a disease which has its basic effect in a disruption of the control of attention, then the reticular system may be the main pathological site."

In my opinion, neither disturbances of attention nor deviations in the level of cortical arousal are at the base of schizophrenia. What is, is an inability to focus attention. This is indeed among the early symptoms of schizophrenia, but, as I will show below, it is secondary to another phenomenon.

A review of the evidence collected by Venables (1966) may demonstrate this. Jasper *et al.* (1939) were able to show that hebephrenics and catatonics have low-amplitude EEGs, while paranoid patients have moderate to high activity in the band of frequencies below 15 cycles per second. Thus it would appear that the nonparanoid patient who is most withdrawn from reality is the patient who gives EEG signs which indicate that he is the most cortically aroused. Goldstein *et al.* (1963, 1965), using a different EEG measure, came to the same conclusion. They measured the variability of the integrated electrical pulses over unit times, and reported an average of coefficient of variation of electrical energy of 15.4 per cent for normals, and 8 per cent for chronic schizophrenics. They deduced that the coefficient of variation of the integration EEG is inversely related to the level of activation; and hence that the chronic schizophrenic is characterized by a state of cortical hyperactivation.

Supporting this view are the studies of Lindemann (1932) and Stevens and Darbyshire (1958). Lindemann found that under sodium amytal, chronic schizophrenics are able to increase contact with the environment. Similarly, Stevens and Derbyshire reported a temporary remission of catatonic symptoms under the influence of barbiturates. This temporary remission was accompanied by a decrease in cortical and autonomic activity shown by changes in EEG, EDG, and EMG indices. Thus, a decrease in withdrawal is accompanied by a decrease in activation.

The third category suggested by Venables is an inferred behavioral finding. Following Lindsley (1958), he hypothesized that the ability to perceive separately pairs of stimuli presented in close temporal proximity might be influenced by activity of the arousal system, and that the better the resolution the higher the degree of activation influencing the cortex. Using this technique, Venables and Wing (1962) found that among nonparanoid schizophrenics, the degree of withdrawal is correlated with the ability to separate pairs of flashes presented at close intervals. The greater the withdrawal, the better the separation of these stimuli—that is, the cortical arousal is higher.

To begin with, these findings are equivocal. Lebedinskaya *et al.* compared the "orientation response" of chronic schizophrenics with that of the acute type. The chronic schizophrenics were characterized by an absence of orientation response. In 9 cases out of 11 the orientation reactions usually did not reveal themselves in any indicator. And these researchers registered a great many indicators: EEGs of the occipital, temporal, sensorimotor and frontal regions, plus a number of other components of the orientation reaction—the vertex potential, the cutaneous-galvanic reflex in the form of the Tarkhanov phenomenon, the PDG, the ECG, pneumograms, oculograms, electrocardiograms, and the motor reactions of the subjects.

Another group of patients who, on the basis of the duration of their illness may be described as acute schizophrenics, and not as chronics, showed very distinct orientation reactions. However, in these cases the extinction of the orienting response was disturbed. They either did not undergo extinction or did so very slowly. On the basis of their data, these researchers state that "It may be taken that the disturbance in the orientation reactions undergoes a regular evolution with deepending of the schizophrenic defect. At first, the orientation reactions become unextinguishable. . . . As the schizophrenic defect deepens, orientation reactions begin to weaken, and this testifies to damage to the reticular formation" (1962, 56).

Venables thinks, then, that chronic schizophrenics are characterized by a high cortical arousal, while Lebedinskaya *et al.* think that they have a low cortical arousal.

Further, the identification of cortical arousal only by means of EEG indices seems to a mistake. Fedio *et al.* (1961) found that schizophrenics, despite their having alpha blockade, an agreed-upon sign of electrographic arousal, failed to show behavioral arousal—that is, a reduced reaction time. Some schizophrenics even performed more slowly. Fedio *et al.* interpreted this finding as evidence of the existence of separate, partially independent neural systems, one mediating behavioral, the other EEG arousal patterns. That is to say, EEG patterns by themselves do not evidence the state of cortical arousal.

Quite in contrast to the evidence collected by Venables, Schooler and Zahn (1968) found that co-operative social interaction both increased arousal and improved performances of chronic nonparanoid schizophrenics. The studies reviewed by Venables show, instead, that a reduction of cortical arousal in chronic schizophrenics is the precondition of improving social contact.

The studies of Lebedinskaya *et al.*, and of Schooler and Zahn show that acute schizophrenics may be in a state of overarousal. In view of this possibility, a suggestion of Callaway (1970) appears convincing. He proposed that schizophrenic thought disorder can be usefully regarded as the result of interference with the running of programs in the human computer. "When schizophrenia is viewed as internal interference with programs, schizophrenic overarousal appears as a result of schizophrenia. This is an interesting alternative to the theory that increased drive is a causal factor in schizophrenia." Indeed, the characteristics of early schizophrenia analyzed so far may be subsumed under internal interference with programs. This internal interference displayed by the retarded auditory reaction time is also instrumental in raising above the optimum the level of cortical arousal, and thereby hampering the focalization of attention.

Hyperaesthesia in early schizophrenia is the outcome of

a constellation peculiar to altered states of consciousness. Usually, there is a positive correlation between the extension of scanning of the visual field and the involuntary, saccadic movements of the eye. Saccadic movements are rapid, flickering jumps of the eye which occur on the average between once and twice a second, even during fixating; they are considered to be essential for detailed vision. Subjects with wide scanning range tend to have higher saccadic rates than subjects with narrower range. However, among altered state subjects—under the influence of psylocybin, LSD, and mescaline—scanning extension and saccadic rates become dissociated, and minimal scanning is accompanied by extraordinarily high saccadic rates. Significantly, this is also the attentional structure of nonparanoid schizophrenics (Hebbard and Fischer, 1966).

Silverman (1968) thinks that this combination is responsible for reports by many altered state subjects of an increased clarity of vision. Restriction and concentration of attention upon a small segment of the field, and a concomitant high saccadic rate apparently causes the brightness of objects to be increased and their physical properties to be accentuated. By disconnecting the usual relations between scanning and rate of saccadic movement of the eye, psychotomimetic drugs accentuate certain segments of the attended field, thereby causing a general hyperaesthesia—which in turn is instrumental in attaching special significance to bodily and mental experiences. In some cases, hyperaesthesia may end up in revelations, conversions, and even in psychotic insight. In this respect there is more than a superficial similarity between schizophrenia and the effects of psychotomimetic drugs. As Ludwig (1966) put it: "I have become very impressed with the predilection of persons in these states to attach an increased meaning or significance to their subjective experiences, ideas or perceptions. . . . In toxic or psychotic states, this increased sense of significance may manifest itself in the attribution of false significance to external cues, ideas of reference and to numerous instances of 'psychotic insight'."

Moreover, psychodelically-drugged subjects also have a significantly retarded auditory reaction time. Their reaction time to light, however, is not impaired as compared with that of normal subjects (Abramson *et al.*, 1955). Is there a causal connection between the delay in auditory reaction time, and the peculiar organization of minimal scanning and extremely high saccadic rate? After all, since I am trying to substantiate the view that a delay in auditory reaction time is the antecedent, and, in a sense, the cause of schizophrenia, it would be rewarding if I could state that hyperaesthesia is also an outcome of the retardation in auditory RT. Alas, I cannot. The connection, if any, between the change in the hierarchical position of auditory RT and the disruption of the usual co-variance between extent of scanning and rate of saccadic eye movement is not yet understood.

The information processing theory of early, nonparanoid schizophrenia, then, views the inability to focalize attention and to elaborate the meaning of the processed information; the thought disturbances; deautomatization; and loss of self-determination as the many consequences of a fateful upheaval in the auditory-verbal modality. The change in the usual hierarchy between auditory and visual RT merely shows such an upheaval without revealing its nature. Notwithstanding this, I would like to hazard the conjecture that the as-yet undiscovered antipsychotic pharmaceutical agent will have to be able to restore the auditory RT of schizophrenics to its premorbid position.

Chapter Six

Psychopathy—
An Old Puzzle
and a New Hope

In Quest of a Definition

CLECKLEY (1950, 1959) listed the major characteristics of a life pattern that in general he considered to be the core of psychopathy. His list includes the following: (1) Unexplained failure. The psychopath inevitably fails in every constructive activity he undertakes. (2) Undisturbed technical intelligence. Nothing is demonstrable in his thinking that accounts for the irrationality of his conduct of life. (3) Absence of neurotic anxiety. He is not handicapped by phobias, obsessions, or hypochondriacal preoccupation. In fact, often he is at ease in many situations where the average person would be tense and apprehensive. (4) Persistent and inadequately motivated antisocial behavior. The psychopath persistently follows a pattern of antisocial behavior that is usually also self-defeating and frustrating to all the aims he claims to pursue. (5) Irresponsibility. He will invariably shrug off his obligations and throw away all that he has gained. (6) Peculiar inability to distinguish between truth and falsehood. Whether there is a good chance that he will get away with a lie or whether detection is almost certain, he shows no sign of perturbation and coolly maintains his position. (7) Inability to accept blame. (8) Failure to learn by experience. (9) Incapacity for love. All his major affective relations evidence astonishing callousness. (10) Inappropriate or fantastic reactions to alcohol. (11) Lack of insight. Cleckley notes that the nature of this limitation was illustrated several times "by brilliant psychopaths, who knew me to be painfully familiar with their astonishing records of dishonesty and irresponsibility, but who nevertheless submitted my name as one to recommend them for positions demanding trustworthiness and stability" (1959, 582). (12) Suicide rarely carried out. (13) Persistent pattern of self-defeat. "One of the truly remarkable features of this life pattern is that a person who shows so concretely the ability to succeed will throw away all he has gained, and apparently what he desires, for no reason comprehensible to others" (1959, 583).

This list of features of psychopathy invites, so to speak, a few critical comments. To begin with, some of these charactcristics arc not specific to psychopathy. For example, threatened suicide, or sham efforts at suicide, sometimes highly dramatic, are not an especially helpful guides for diagnosing psychopathy. Actually, most people would consider this hysterical rather than psychopathic behavior. Similarly, a failure to learn by experience confronts us everywhere. A phobic patient will never "learn" by experience, and will stick to his counter measures; a masochistic patient will not "learn" from the degradations he has suffered, and will repeat his characteristic behavior until a psychotherapeutic intervention succeeds in reshaping his psychic make-up. Unexplained failures and a persistent pattern of self-defeat are also not specifically psychopathic.

Furthermore, some of these individual characteristics

can be grouped together—for example, incapacity for love and shallow, impersonal responses to sexual life. An inability to distinguish between truth and falsehood, lack of insight, inability to accept blame, and irresponsibility also form a single group. Thus, after we eliminate those symptoms which are also present in neurotics, and reorganize the conceptual frame, we have the following major symptoms which delineate psychopathy as a special entity: incapacity for love; inability to accept blame (including under this rubric the characteristics of inability to distinguish between truth and falsehood, lack of insight, and irresponsibility); and being driven by impulses, as evidenced by inadequately motivated antisocial behavior. These, in concert, comprise and define the nucleus of psychopathic behavior. One or another of these manifestations may strike the observer at different times; but the simultaneous appearance of all these symptoms is the basis for a diagnosis of psychopathy.

We have now to confront an intriguing question. Are these enumerated constituents independent factors, or is one of them perhaps the primary disturbance and the others its consequences? I suggest a compromise: that the incapacity for love and the state of being driven by impulses are independent factors, and the inability to accept blame is a consequence of both these symptoms.

The impulse-driven personality

Impulsiveness means a lack of control. Usually, it is assumed that impulses and their control are the functions of different psychic systems: the control is ego-syntonic, and the impulses are ego-alien. This conventional understanding of impulsiveness is borne out by self-observation. One may be struck, once in a while, by having done or said something not consistent with one's self-esteem. While not doubting the genuineness of surprise one may feel in such confrontations with oneself, I would like to emphasize that impulsiveness does not necessitate the assumption of a conflict between instinctual drives and defenses. In point of fact, it is better understood as a peculiarity of information processing. Such a conclusion is implicated in Petrie's (1967) continuum of reducer-moderate-augmenter.

As will be recalled, in the kinesthetic aftereffect experiment the subject is blindfolded and feels the width of a measuring block with the thumb and forefinger of the right hand. Then, with the thumb and forefinger of his other hand, he feels a long tapered bar and determines on the bar the place where it seems to be the same width as the measuring block. Afterwards, he rubs a wider stimulating block with his right thumb and forefinger. After 90 seconds of rubbing, he is again given the original measuring block and tapered bar and compares them as before. The width experienced now by different subjects will be distributed on a continuum of augmentation-reduction; the measuring block is experienced by the extreme reducer as half its original size, and by the extreme augmenter as half again as large. Co-varying with these individual differences in sensory experiences, augmenters' pain threshold is low, while that of the reducers' is high.

The important point for our discussion here is that Petrie found a deviant in her typology, the so-called stimulus-governed type. These individuals (according to Petrie, 20 per cent of the juvenile delinquents) are characterized by an exaggerated contrast effect, as measured by sensory aftereffects. That is, after having rubbed a large block, such a subject will reduce the experienced size of the measuring bar; the opposite effect occurs after rubbing a small block. The great majority, be they reducers or augmenters, possess a stable mode of processing these stimuli; but stimulus-governed persons who experience extreme swings from expansion to contraction are completely at the mercy of their immediate environment. They are pulled from one extreme to the other without being aided by an internal stabilizer; their behavior is changeable and unpredictable. This unpredictability (the essence of what is called impulsiveness), however, is a consequence of their being stimulus-governed. They are impulsive not because of the weakness of their ego or the strength of their instinctual drives, but rather because they lack a stable way to process information. It would thus be more correct to label them situationally-determined instead of impulse-driven persons.

I would like to suggest that such a deficiency of control impairs the "me-ness" quality of their experiences, and thus determines to a large extent their ability to take responsibility for their own deeds.

The conception of "me-ness," as used here, is a contribution of Claparède (1911). Analyzing the memory performances of a korsakow patient, Claparède maintained that "recognition" is only made possible by an accompanying feeling of "me-ness"; a chain of fitting associations may subserve adaptive behaviour, but it does not suffice to produce recognition. In one experiment, while shaking hands with a female patient suffering from korsakow syndrome, Claparède pricked her hand with a pin hidden between his fingers. The light pain was as quickly forgotten as indifferent perceptions. But when he again reached out for her hand, she pulled it back. When asked for the reason, she answered evasively, "Doesn't one have the right to withdraw her hand?" Pressed further, she said, "Is there perhaps a pin hidden in your hand?" To the question, "What makes you suspect me of wanting to stick you?" she answered, "That was an idea that went through my mind." Then she said, "Sometimes pins are hidden in people's hands"; but never would she "recognize" the experimenter as the one who stuck her.

When told a story, this patient seemed not to remember it, not even the fact that someone had read to her. In fact, however, appropriate questions could elicit some of those "lost" items. But the point is that those retrieved items were not "recognized" by her as such, but rather, were thought to be ideas which, by chance, had gone through her mind. What this patient was suffering from was clearly not a total inability to register and learn—it was "an isolated destruction of the 'me-ness'," as Claparède put it. Indeed, although she asserted that she did not recognize her nurse, who had been with her for six months, the patient soon after asked her whether dinner time was near. Thus, the korsakow syndrome is a disease of "me-ness" rather than of registering. Many of the seemingly not remembered impressions are available to korsakow patients; but they occur in an incidental, automatic manner without any feeling of familiarity.

Claparède thought that the hypothesis of "me-ness," which accounts for the fact that loss of recognition is generally accompanied by loss of voluntary recall, also explained some posthypnotic phenomena. Instructions received while one is hypnotized are performed by remembering, and not by recalling—that is, without the feeling of "me-ness." These instructions are not voluntarily recallable, and when they do emerge, it as though they come from alien, dissociated, psychic realms not united with the normal "me." Sleep learning also corroborates the consequences of a failing "me-ness." Learning, apparently, can take place during sleep. On awakening, however, such learning will be experienced "as a thought of which the source remained outside consciousness. . . . it is as if it belonged to an alien personality" (Svyadoshch, 1968).

Let us now come back to the impulse-driven people whose behavior is situationally determined. Since many of their deeds are not planned or controlled, but rather are unforeseen or unpredictable even to themselves, the question arises whether these deeds can be recognized later on as belonging to their "me." In this connection, Redl and Wineman (1951) have made an important observation about "the evaporation of self-contributed links in the causal chain" in juvenile delinquents. Though the young delinquents they studied had many defensive alibis, Redl and Wineman thought that sometimes they were not lying. Unless they were reminded of what they had done immediately afterwards, their recollection of what had happened a short time before was actually obliterated in the deluge of its aftermath. The child who is inconsolable over a broken toy is often really unable to recall the fury with which he had mishandled and broken it; he only sees the breaking as an accident.

In the opinion of Redl and Wineman, this fast "evaporation rate" for their own contributions to the causal chain is actually one of the most serious obstacles to psychotherapy with these youngsters. What, then, is the reason for this evaporation rate? It seems plausible to assume that such an evaporation is particular to experiences which once were thought to be registered in a "hypnoid" state

of mind, devoid of "me-ness." In other words, those experiences are not voluntarily recallable, not because of a
motive opposing them, but rather because of a failure to
integrate them into the conscious self.

But, if these young delinquents were impeded in planning and controlling their own behavior, could not such
experiences determine their outlook on the causes of
their behavior? If their behavior is not self-controlled, it
is only a small step further for them to shrug off responsibility for all their actions. We have to reckon with the fact
that such people are not disposed to experience remorse
or shame. Their very psychic make-up blocks insight.

As far as the psychopath's inability to establish love
relationships is concerned, there seems to be a consensus
that underlying this phenomenon is a defective early
mother-child relationship. For example, Powdermaker *et
al.* (1937) described a group of young delinquents who
were asocial but not obviously neurotic, with whom no
treatment method worked. Common to all of them was an
inability to establish an emotional tie with any member of
the staff. The outstanding feature of their life stories was,
according to the authors, their having had no opportunity
to enjoy satisfactory libidinal relationships in their early
childhoods.

Bowlby (1946) similarly described a group of young delinquents, the so-called affectionless characters. These
youngsters suffered complete and prolonged separation
(six months or more) from their mothers or established
foster-mothers during their first year of life. This prolonged break in the mother-child relationship during the
early critical period left a characteristic impression on
their personalities, namely, an emotional isolation. They
failed to develop libidinal ties with other children or with

adults, and consequently had no friendships.

It is apparent that being driven by impulses and the inability to love are independent basic factors. The first is the outcome of a peculiar mode of information processing, as exemplified by the stimulus-governed variant of Petrie's typology. The second is rooted in individual life experiences. The common denominator of these independent factors is the curious fact that both of them, separately, may lead to a lack of remorse. An individual who is only impulse driven may belatedly feel remorse, but the one who is both impulse-driven *and* incapable of loving will not know what guilt feelings are.

A Remedy

The affectionless characters described by Bowlby are, to use his term, hard-boiled. To these lost souls it seems a matter of indifference whether they are in favor with others or not. Since they are unable to establish genuine emotional relations, the state of a relationship at a given moment lacks all meaning for them. Understandably, most clinicians are rather skeptical regarding the chances of psychotherapy with psychopaths. However, the inability to love is only one of the basic features of psychopathy, and our failure in improving it must not deter us from further attempts. Instead, we should turn our attention to the second basic feature, that of being driven by impulse.

The most striking experience of an impulse-driven individual is his lack of control over his own behavior: he cannot anticipate the results of his deeds, and therefore cannot learn from his experience. He is, in a sense, justified in shrugging off every responsibility for the outcome of what he does. The therapeutic approach with the psychopath should concentrate on getting him to gain control over his actions. It is conceivable that the very experience of mastery will help him not only in anticipating the results of his deeds, but will support him in conducting a socially acceptable life, even before any repair of the further basic defect, that is, his inability to establish emotional relations.

Bio-feedback is a recent approach which promises what hitherto seemed to be beyond our power. Blood pressure, blood flow, heart rate, lymph flow, muscle tension, brainwaves—all these have already been self-regulated through training. Where is the limit to this capacity for self-regulation? Many researchers think that any body process can be controlled in some degree. Bio-feedback, to use the fortunate term of Hefferline (1971), means control of what was thought to be uncontrollable.

Among the many reports on the possibilities of self-control, Miller's (1969) experiments are perhaps the most instructive, because his subjects were rats. Despite the limits of communication necessary in establishing bio-feedback, these animals acquired an amazing degree of control over their autonomic functions. Miller's basic technical problem was how to rule out the possibility that the animal had learned some skeletal response which in turn could produce control of the viscera. The assumption of such a mediation was the usual objection of sceptics to reports of voluntary control over the viscera. For instance, Kimble (1961) thought that, "Yoga procedures which provide the most impressive examples of voluntary control over involuntary responses suggest that . . . the involuntary responses are controlled indirectly through skeletal mechanism." In his opinion, voluntary control of vasomotor responses, the GSR, and pulse retardation might require only that the subject become a little tense to acquire control over the autonomic process. Therefore Miller and his co-workers paralyzed rats by curare. The curare blocks acetylcholine, the chemical transmitter by which cerebrospinal nerve impulses are delivered to skeletal muscles, but does not interfere with consciousness or with the transmitters that mediate autonomic responses.

In one of their experiments, half of the paralyzed rats were rewarded by electrical stimulation of the brain whenever their heart rate was above normal. The two groups showed highly reliable changes in the direction of the reward. They were also able to control the increase and decrease of blood pressure, intestinal contractions, blood vessel diameter, and rate of urine formation. Further, the paralyzed rat can learn to control its blood vessels independently of general changes in heart rate and blood pressure. Rats rewarded for relatively greater vasoconstriction in the right ear obtained the required effect, and so did rats rewarded for a change in the opposite direction.

This sounds almost unbelievable, but they are hard facts. Experiments on human subjects, which permitted communication about the subjective experiences accompanying the learning of self-control, made plausible the unbelievable. Peper (1971) let half of his subjects receive a high feedback tone when alpha occurred in the right hemisphere, while the other half of the subjects received the high feedback tone when alpha occurred in the left hemisphere. A low tone was received when alpha happened to be generated in the other hemisphere. The subject who was capable of the required control reported that to keep alpha on the right hemisphere she spelled things, named the American states, and multiplied high figures. She kept alpha on the left hemisphere by singing and feeling the rhythm of dancing.

This subject relied intuitively on the localization of cerebral functions demonstrated by Sperry (1968) in his split brain studies. That is to say, this subject, by verbalizing, activated the left hemisphere, thus allowing relatively more alpha on the right side; conversely, by singing she suppressed alpha waves on the right side. Most probably, there are many more ways of subserving the expansion of voluntary control.

If it is possible to train control over visceral functions, we may perhaps also succeed in teaching our psychopaths to control their impulsivity. Our armamentarium for treating psychopaths is extremely modest; why not take advantage of the opportunities offered by this new technique? True, control over motor units or visceral functions is not a remedy specific to psychopathy; however, if young psychopaths can learn voluntary control over these functions, they may gain a sense of mastery over themselves to which they are not accustomed. Cloward and Ohlin (1960) observed that the most important step in the withdrawal of sentiments supporting the legitimacy of conventional norms is the attribution of the cause of failure to the others. Maybe the experience of controlling their own bodies will enable psychopaths to change their usual attribution of causation, a development which then might be exploited as the basis for a psychotherapy vainly sought for until now.

Chapter Seven

Scaffolding
For A Theory
of Psychopathology

What Psychology Is About

KOCH (1959) OPENS his textbook with the following comment. *"Psychology: A Study of Science* is a report of investigations into the nature and tendency of a roughly definable cluster of human knowledge-seeking activities known as psychological science." That is to say, psychology is a report of investigations into what is known as psychological science. We may ask, however, to whom is it so known?

Hilgard and Atkinson (1967) define psychology as the science that studies the behavior of man and other animals. By behavior they mean (and this is the crucial point) those activities of an organism that can be observed by another or by an experimenter's instruments. In Hebb's (1966) view, what psychology is essentially about is an understanding of man's mind and behavior. Krech *et al.* (1969), very much like Koch, evade confronting the problem—their textbook contains no definition of psychology.

The behavioristic approach, exemplified here by Hilgard and Atkinson, suffers from a logical deficiency. Behavior defined as activities observed by another legitimizes in disguised form the very aspect which behaviorism thought to make absolute, namely, subjective experiences. My observation and report of a subject's behavior are as subjective as his observations and report of his own behavior.

Razran (1961) unwittingly stated the paradox inherent in behaviorism in the title of one of his papers: *The Observable Unconscious and the Inferrable Conscious.* Head over heels, indeed.

In point of fact, the observer is not in need of any inferences concerning his own activities. He need only recognize, as he indeed does, that the fellow under observation is like himself, and he arrives at Hebb's definition: psychology's domain is man's mind and observable behavior.

Nevertheless we are indebted to behaviorism because of its emphasis on observable behavior. In describing behavior one describes an organism in its environment while the concept of mind can easily lead one astray into intrapsychic realms. As a matter of fact, Freud and Jung, by overstressing instinctual drives or archetypes, did their best, each in his own way, to undervalue the impact of interactions between man and his environment. Although Freud recognized by implication at least that an instinct is an action pattern devised to be actualized in a living environment, he nullified this insight by his invention of the "vicissitudes" of the drive. A sexual urge which can "flow" backward, thus increasing narcissism, or upwards, thus generating sublimated cultural interests—

such a conception invites, indeed, obliges one to turn his attention to metapsychology rather than to psychology.

Accustomed to the world of emotions and fantasies, psychodynamically-oriented clinicians cannot help becoming less interested in the environment of their patients. The consequence of such a focusing on dynamics was pointed out by Grinker *et al.:* "Apparently, in spite of specifically looking for behavioral traits, our interests and familiarity with content of thoughts and feelings interfere with our observation of what goes on in front of us. Paradoxically we can see and communicate better what we have to interpret and infer" (1961, 80).

It is important to emphasize that what mental functioning subserves is interaction with environment; life phenomena are only understandable when we are aware of the incessantly ongoing exchange and interaction between an organism and its environment. Even when there is no interference with food intake, elimination, sleeping, or temperature, merely preventing sensory input will cause dramatic changes in the subject's psychic make-up. He is not able to concentrate, to think coherently; some subjects report hallucinations, feelings of unreality, and anxiety approaching panic. Plainly, a human being while awake is programmed to interact with the environment. The primacy given to exteroception over interoception is a logical sequel of this interaction. Indeed, Mészáros (1965) was able to show the existence of such a rank order in registering information. Visceral afferent nerves are allowed to transmit their impulses only between strict limits. With increasing duration of the impulses transmitted by them, the amplitude of the evoked potential decreases and the duration of the response becomes shorter. While the receptivity of the cortex to such stimuli is provisionally diminished under the same circumstances, impulses of external origin are facilitated. This difference proves convincingly the high relevance of interaction with environment to our psychic make-up.

The Control of Behavior

People sometimes behave like an arrow shot from the bow, reacting with reflex speed and resolution. Other times, people behave like fumblers in the dark, for example, when trying to recall a forgotten name. If I am not mistaken, W. James (1890) was the first psychologist in modern times to analyze these situations. This is his description: "The state of our consciousness is peculiar. There is a gap therein; but no mere gap. It is a gap that is intensely active . . . If wrong names are proposed to us, this singularly definite gap acts immediately so as to negate them. They do not fit into its mould. . . . The rhythm of a lost word may be there without a sound to clothe it. . . ." The gap James was talking about is indeed a peculiar one. It is now better known as the tip-of-the-tongue phenomenon. Curiously enough, the subject seems to know what he apparently does not know. How can we explain that one is able to judge the relation of the suggested word to the sought-for word while failing to verbalize it? Similarly, how can we explain that when the eye muscles are paralyzed, an intended movement, though failing, will result in perceiving of the visual world jumping in the direction of the intended movement? These phenomena are only understandable if we hypothesize with Holst (1950, 1954) the existence of efference copies. Every intention produces an efference copy which is matched with the feedback of the sequential performance. When there is congruence between the information fed back and the efference copy, the latter will be inhibited and fade away. If, however, due to the paralysis of eye muscles the efference-copy will not be matched by any reafference, the intended but unfulfilled eye movement will result in the illusion of a movement of the surroundings in the same direction.

This formulation is close to the revision of the concept of a reflex proposed by Miller *et al.* (1960): Test-Operate-Test-Exit (TOTE), up to a crucial point. The TOTE is conceived as a servomechanism, and it does not account for intention. Here is how Pribram puts this view: "To be effective, input must be compared to and tested against spontaneous or corollary central neural activity; the results of this comparison initiate some operation. . . . The consequences of this operation are then fed back to the comparator and the loop continues until the test has been satisfied—until some previous setting, indicative of the state-to-be-achieved, has been attained (exit)" (1971, 93).

The reflex arc "fiction" (as Pribram calls it) cannot encompass the data that demonstrate the central control of input mechanisms; this is why it should be replaced by the TOTE fiction. The statement quoted above does indeed begin by describing this central control of input. It ends, however by pointing out a "state-to-be-achieved." A state to be achieved hints at an intention which precedes input, but the TOTE servomechanism is conceived as initiated only by input performances.

TOTE as it stands has a Janus face. It grants the organism, by means of the central control of input, an extent of freedom alien to the reflex-arc conception, but it restricts this freedom by being initiated only by input performances. This is a faint echo of reflexology-behaviorism, which envisages a passive organism activated by stimuli working upon it. Anokhin, while himself not indifferent to this background, nevertheless did not hesitate to conclude ". . . that only the afferentation stops further reflex acts which correspond to the *intention* that generated the reflex act, or, speaking physiologically, the return afferentation just corresponds to *some ready complex of excitations which had arisen before the reflex act took place"* (1966, 82). Clearly, an interaction between the organism and its environment presupposes two active partners of equal standing. Both mind and external factors participate in enacting the drama of living. A theory of mind must be broad enough to do justice to a powerful environment as well as to an active, striving organism which has needs, intentions, and attitudes; to programmed performances, as well as to inventions.

Let us state again that behavior initiated by the organism is guided by the comparing of the sequences of performance with the efference copy. Once initiated, an action does not continue forever; after a while it is inhibited. Diamond *et al.* (1963) suggest this agreed-upon fact should be called Haidenhain's principle. Bubnoff and Haidenhain (1883) were the first to realize that every cortical excitation tends to arouse a local inhibitory process which has the function of limiting the excitation. While Haidenhain's principle, a beautiful variant of Hegelian dialectics, does not prefer excitation over inhibition, physiologists did prefer the investigation of excitation. Diamond *et al.* remark that Sherrington's great work, *The Integrative Action of the Nervous System,* might just as well have been called *The Importance of Inhibition for Nervous Integration.* "But it was not so titled, and physiologists somehow succeeded in recognizing all the facts relating to posture and locomotion without drawing implications for their wider significance." (1963, 5).

Let us therefore pay due attention to inhibition, and follow up the psychological aspects of terminating an action. Theories of behavior which assume the existence of psychical energy conceive of the initiation and termination of an action as resulting from an increase and decrease of that energy or drive. Sexual intercourse is paradigmatic for a behavior terminated due to consummation, that is, drive reduction. A game of football, on the other hand, ends because a whistle blows, not because the players' energy is exhausted; or, to borrow an example from Bowlby (1969), a baby may cease to cry when he sees his mother and resume soon afterward when she disappears from sight. In this case, the cessation of crying and its resumption are obviously not caused by first a drop and then a rise in the amount of psychical energy available, but rather by the meaning of a sign. Except for intercourse and sleep, a usual day is filled with activities the termination of which is due to information received, like finishing a lecture at an agreed-upon time, or stopping the car at a red light. That is to say, cognition is generally, though not exclusively, responsible for terminating an action.

This simple survey of the conditions for terminating an action may appear to contradict the perspective one gets by analyzing the initiation of behavior. A second look, however, indicates that in fact they are convergent.

If we ask ourselves why we act, our answer must include the reason for a change in the previous situation. This can be the pressure of a need, or the impact of an external force activating the organism. If we emphasize one of these possibilities and neglect the other, we can develop either a motivational theory of behavior or one of the variants of reflexology. Reflexology emphasizes necessity: ". . . a stimulus appears to connected with a definite response, as cause with effect. . . . It follows from all this that *instincts and reflexes are alike the inevitable responses of the organism to the internal and external stimuli"* (Pavlov, 1927). Motives, on the other hand, are understood as steering forces which drive the organism to do its best, but are not so compelling as a reflex arc.

Unlike a reflex, which is said to be an inevitable reaction, a motive points out a goal the attainment of which may demand detours, retreats, and many more maneuvers—in one word, cognition. In spite of this, many theories of motivation keep motives and cognition apart. For instance, Freud hypothesized two psychic systems, one only for motivating and another only for controlling. However, if a motive is conceived of as not being synonymous with a reflex, then its very definition implies cognitive control. An analysis of the conditions responsible for terminating actions leaves little doubt that cognition is, indeed, the main control system of behavior.

Whether the control system in charge is cognition or servomechanism, behavior is always sequentially actualized, the unfolding of one phase preparing the way for the next one. This sequential actualization depends on a smooth flow of information feedback about the results of action already completed. Any disturbance in the feedback of information will inevitably impair the control of behavior. For example, Dinnerstein *et al.* (1962) suggest that a delayed feedback of proprioception can explain at least some of the patterns constituting Parkinson's disease.

Parkinson's involves a loss of normal synchrony between agonist and antagonist musculature, ending in muscle rigidity, tremor, and slow movement. Dinnerstein *et al.* hypothesize that if transmission of the proprioceptive impulses is excessively delayed, the initial automatic movement will be large because the antagonistic muscle contraction would be delayed. The sequence of delayed proprioceptive impulses and prolonged compensating muscle contractions would produce hyperactivity in the gamma system (one of the contractile systems of muscles) with resulting muscle rigidity.

Furthermore, it is wellknown that an experimentallycaused delay in auditory feedback—that is, in hearing one's own voice—leads to a prolongation of vowels, repetition of consonants, increased intensity of utterance, mispronounciations, substitutions, often an omission of word endings, and many more changes (Lee, 1951; Yates, 1963).

Similarly, I suggest that a delay in the auditory-verbal modality is the immediate antecedent of the symptomatology of early nonparanoid schizophrenia. In contrast to normal subjects, nonparanoid schizophrenics' auditory reaction time is retarded as compared with their own RT to visual stimuli. Using this curious change in the usual rank order of sensory modalities as the point of departure, it is possible to explain schizophrenic symptoms from deautomatization through processing of meaning to disturbances of attention.

I would like to stress that a systematic follow up of the central control of behavior may open new vistas for our understanding of psychopathology and therapy. At a time when psychologists and physiologists seemed not to care much about the concept of feedback, the philosopher Scheler (1928) stated that consciousness emerges out of

the pain of the discrepancy between a plan and the difficulties of actualizing it. Control of behavior by means of
feedback is the precondition of consciousness in animals,
and also the reason for its absence in plants, Scheler argued. Although he was mistaken here (some machines, as
well as animals, are equipped with servomechanisms)
Scheler nevertheless did sense the value of the feedback
concept for a theory of behavior, for his statement essentially means that the development of feedback information is a precondition for the emergence of consciousness.

Slightly modifying Scheler's intuition, I would like to
suggest that consciousness is to be postulated in living
organisms if a central control of behavior is accompanied
by the capacity for feeling. Or rather, I should say if the
central control of behavior is *followed* by the ability to
feel, for the development of feelings can only follow, not
precede, central control of behavior. This view is supported by an experiment of Schachter and Singer (1962),
which indicates that it is the meaning of the situation that
determines the quality of feeling. These researchers
showed that while under the influence of an adrenaline
injection, subjects experienced hostile or friendly feelings
in accordance with their actual social situations. Adrenaline only intensified both friendly and hostile feelings; the
quality of the feeling itself was determined by the meaning of the situation.

Clearly, the popular concept of a natural conflict between feelings and cognition (heart and intelligence) has
no foundation. Feelings do not reflect the functioning of
an autonomic nervous system as opposed to a voluntary,
rational nervous system. One of the most important results of the work in bio-feedback is the conclusion that we
must give up this differentiation. What was thought to be

autonomic is, in fact, cortically represented and is potentially under voluntary control.

Summing up, then, we may say, first, that behavior consists of sequentially performed phases; and second, that its actualization is mainly cognitively controlled, and consequently any derangement of this control will cause a disturbance of behavior.

Disorders of Behavior

The majority of the known categories of psychopathology are to be explained as disturbances of the central control of behavior. I have suggested that a delay in the auditory-verbal modality, most probably of the feedback process, is the last factor in the chain of causation of nonparanoid schizophrenia, and similarly, that psychopathic behavior may be understood as an outcome of a peculiarity of information processing. It is characteristic of stimulus-governed persons (Petrie, 1967) that many of their actions are performed in a hypnoid state, that is, they do not plan them and cannot control them. Experiences registered while one is in a hypnoid state lack the quality of "me-ness" (Claparède, 1911), and are therefore not available for voluntary recall. This lack of recall was described by Redl and Wineman (1946) as the main obstacle to psychotherapy intended to help such patients gain insight into their own motives.

Freud explained the post-traumatic state as a failure to control the intensity of input. While agreeing with Freud, I would like to stress that understimulation destroys the central control of behavior just as overstimulation does. For example, epileptic attacks tend to occur under both of these conditions. It seems a matter of common sense to assume that stress and fatigue can trigger an attack; but as Lennox (1960) states, "Vacancy of mind is fuel for seizure of all kinds." He also quotes patients' claims that they can ward off an epileptic attack by keeping busy with an intellectual task. And sensory deprivation can be as harmful and damaging to central control as a surplus of stimuli. Obsessional states, while not yet fully understood, also point to a failure of control. Haidenhain's (1881) principle, that every cortical excitation tends to arouse a local inhibitory process which has the function of limiting the excitation, leads us to expect that an action initiated will soon be terminated. Obsessional patients fail to terminate their ruminations or some of their activities. Even if their obsessions turn out to have a symbolic meaning, the core-phenomenon of this disease is the inability to stop those actions after a while. By investigating the conditions responsible for this failure, instead of concentrating on the symbolic meaning of the rituals, we may be able to clarify the nature of the obsessional states and so work toward an appropriate remedy.

In Freud's view, sexual disorders are the outcome of a conflict between the urge to satisfaction and a resistance to that urge originating in anxiety. Significantly, Freud's theory stresses the initiation of behavior, which he understood to be the consequence of an accumulation of instinctual drives; yet, while granting anxiety a central place in controlling behavior, he made explicit the cognitive aspect of behavior. Anxiety means an evaluation of information; anxiety is always preceded by processes of cognition.

What sexual disorders demonstrate, then, is that even if the chain of events begins with the push of an instinctual drive, it is not possible to analyze behavior by separating motives from their control systems, and by paying

exclusive attention to drives and their assumed vicissitudes.

Unlike sexual disorders, where Freud's approach appears immediately convincing, depression is understandable only as an outcome of object relationships. Being
abandoned and helpless is the precondition of depression,
rather than a thwarted sexual urge or aggressive drive.
But helplessness, like anxiety, is the consequence of an
assessment of one's situation, that is, of cognition.

The brief glance at the major fields of psychopathology
presented in this small book does not claim to be a full
elaboration of a cognitive viewpoint. Rather, it is an invi-
tation to join in the task of integrating the theory of
psychopathology and the practice of psychotherapy with
the disciplines of processing information.

Bibliography

Abramson, H.A., Yarvik, M.E., Kaufman, M.R., Kornetsky, C., Levine, A. and Wagner, M. "Lysergic Acid Diethylamide (LSD-25): Physiological and Perceptual Responses," *Journal of Psychology*, 39 (1955), 3–60.

Adam, G. *Interoception and Behavior.* Budapest, Adademai Kiado, 1967.

Alexander, F. *Psychosomatic Medicine.* New York, Norton, 1950.

Amster, H. "Semantic Satiation and Generation," *Psychological Bulletin*, 62 (1964), 273–86.

Annett, E. *Feedback and Human Behaviour.* London, Penguin Books, 1969.

Anokhin, P.K. "Special Features of Different Apparatus of the Conditioned Reflex and their Importance to Psychology: Report to Conference on Psychology, 1955," in A. Leontyev, A. Luirya, and A. Smirov (eds.), *Psychological Research in the U.S.S.R.* Moscow, Progress, 1966.

Aschaffenburg, G. "Die Ideenflucht," *Psychologische Studien*, 1902.

Ashby, W. R. "Energy and Signal," *International Journal of Neuroscience*, 1 (1970), 95–98.

Bartlett. *Remembering: A Study in Experimental and Social Psychology.* London, Cambridge University Press, 1932.

Basmajian, R. "Electromyography Comes of Age," *Science*, 176 (1972), 603–09.

Bateson, J. "Exchange of Information about Patterns of Human Behavior," in W. S. Fields, and W. Abbott (eds.), *Information Storage and Neural Control.* Springfield, Ill., Charles Thomas, 1963.

Benjamin, T. B., and Watt, N.F. "Psychopathology and Semantic Interpretation of Ambiguous Words." Unpublished manuscript quoted in B. Maher, "The Language of Schizophrenia: A Review and Interpretation," *British Journal of Psychiatry*, 120 (1972), 3–17.

Bergson, H. "Le rêve," *Revue Scientifique*, 1901.

———— "L'effort mental," *Revue Scientifique*, 1902.

Betleheim, S. and Hartman, H. "On Parapraxes in the Korsakow Psychosis" (1924), in D. Rapaport (ed.), *Organization and Pathology of Thought.* New York, Columbia University Press, 1951.

Bettelheim, B. *The Informed Heart.* London, Thames and Hudson, 1960.

Binswanger, L. "The Case of Ellen West," in R. May, E. Angel, and F. Ellenberger (eds.), *Existence: A New Dimension in Psychiatry and Psychology.* New York, Basic Books, 1958.

Bleuler, E. *Dementia Praecox or the Group of Schizophrenias* (1911). New York, International Universities Press, 1950.

Bleuler, M. "A 23-year Longitudinal Study of 208 Schizophrenics and Impressions in Regard to the Nature of Schizophrenia," in D. Rosenthal, and S. S. Kety (eds.), *The Transmission of Schizophrenia*. London, Pergamon Press, 1968.

Blum, G.S., Geiwitz, P.J., and Havenstein, L.S. "Principles of Cognitive Reverberation," *Behavioral Science*, 12 (1967), 275–88.

Blum, G. S., Havenstein, L.S., and Graef, J.R., "Studies in Cognitive Reverberation, Replications and Extensions," *Behavioral Science*, 13 (1968), 171–77.

Bower, G. H., "A Multidimensional Theory of the Memory Trace," in K. W. Spence, and J. T. Spence (eds.), *The Psychology of Learning and Motivation*. New York, Academic Press, I1, 229–35.

Bowlby, Y. *Attachment and Loss*. London, Hogarth Press, 1969.

Bowlby, Y. *Forty-four Juvenile Thieves, Their Characters and Homelife*. London, Hogarth Press, 1946.

Breuer, J., and Freud, S. "On Hysterical Mechanism" (1892). *Collected Papers*, VI, 1924.

Bronovski, Y. and Bellugi, U. "Language, Name, and Concept," *Science* 168 (1970), 669–73.

Brown, R., and McNeill, D. "The 'Tip of the Tongue' Phenomenon," *Journal of Verbal Learning and Verbal Behavior*, 5 (1965), 325–37.

Bruner, J.S., "On Perceptual Readiness," *Psychological Bulletin*, 64, 123–52.

Bruner, J.S., "Ueber die Willenshandlungen und ihre Hierarchische Struktur," in A. Koestler, and J.R. Smythies (eds.), *Das Neue Menschenbild*. Zurich, Molden, 1970.

Bryden, M.P., "Attentional Strategies and Short-term Memory in Dichotic Listening," *Cognitive Psychology*, 2 (1971), 99–116.

Bubnoff, W., and Haidenhain, R., (1881) "Uber Erregungs, und Hemmungsvorgange innerhalb der motorischen Hirvzentren," *Pflungers Archiv des gesammten Physiologie*, 26, 137–200.

Buchsbaum, M., "Neural Events and the Psychophysical Law," *Science*, 170 (1974), 1044.

Callaway, E. "Schizophrenia and Interference: An Analogy with a Malfunctioning Computer," in R. Cancro (ed.), *The Schizophrenic Syndrome*. New York, Bruner/Mazel, 1971.

Cameron, N. "Reasoning, Regression, and Communication in Schizophrenics," *Psychological Monographs*, 1938.

————. "An Experimental Analysis of Schizophrenic Thinking," in J.S. Kasanin (ed.), *Language and Thought in Schizophrenia*. Berkeley, California University Press, 1944.

Cancro, R. (ed.). *Menninger Foundation Conference on the Schizophrenic Syndrome.* New York, Bruner/Mazel, 1970.

Capstick, N. "Anafranil in Obsessional States: A Follow-up Study," presented at 5th World Congress of Psychiatry, Mexico, 1971.

Chapman, L.Y., Chapman, Y.P., and Miller, G.A. "A Theory of Verbal Behavior in Schizophrenia," in B. Maher (ed.), *Progress in Experimental Personality Research,* New York, Academic Press, 1964.

Claparède, E. (1911) "Recognition and 'Me-ness' " (1911), in D. Rapaport (ed.), *Organization and Pathology of Thought.* New York, Columbia University Press, 1951.

Cleckley, H.M. *The Mask of Sanity,* St. Louis, Mosby, 1955.

———. "Psychopathic States", in S. Arieti (ed.), *American Handbook of Psychiatry.* New York, Basic Books, 1959.

Cloward, R. A., and Ohlin, L.E. *Delinquency and Opportunity: A Theory of Delinquent Groups.* Glencoe, Ill., Free Press, 1960.

Conrad, R. "The Chronology of the Development of Covert Speech in Children," *Child Development,* 5 (1971), 398–405.

Destrooper, J., and Broughton, R. "REM Awakening Latencies and a Possible REM Breakthrough Phenomenon," *Psychophysiology,* 6 (1969), 216.

Diamond, S., Balvin, R.S., and Diamond, F.R. *Inhibition and choice: A Neurobehavioral Approach to Problems of Plasticity in Behavior.* New York, Harper and Row, 1963.

Dinnerstein, A.J., Frigyesi, T., and Lowenthal, M. "Delayed Feedback as a Possible Mechanism in Parkinsonism," *Perceptual and Motor Skills,* 15 (1962), 667–80.

Eccles, J.C., in *Brain Mechanisms and Learning,* a symposium organized by C.I.O.M.C. Oxford, Blackwell, 1961.

Ellis, H. "On Dreaming of the Dead" (1889), *Psychological Review,* 2.

Evarts, E.V. "Activity of Neurons in Visual Cortex of the Cat during Sleep with Low Voltage Fast EEG Activity," *Journal of Neurophysiology,* 25 (1962), 812–16.

Fairbairn, W.R. "On Hysterical Mechanisms," *British Journal of Medical Psychology,* 27 (1954), 105–25.

Fedio, P., Mirsky, A.F., Smith, W.J., and Parry, D. "Reaction Time and EEG Activation in Normal and Schizophrenic Subjects," *EEG and Clinical Neurophysiology,* 13 (1961), 923–26.

Fenichel, O. *Outline of Clinical Psychoanalysis.* New York, W.W. Norton, 1934.

———. *The Psychoanalytic Theory of Neurosis.* New York, W. W. Norton, 1945.

Festinger, L. *A Theory of Cognitive Dissonance.* Stanford, Stanford University Press, 1957.

Fishbein, W., Tusa, R.Y., and McGaugh. "The Effect of REM Deprivation during the Retention Interval on Long-Term Memory," *Psychophysiology*, 7 (1971), 299.

Fiss, H., Klein, G.S., and Bokert, E. "Waking Fantasies Following Interruption of Two Types of Sleep," *Archives of General Psychiatry*, 14 (1966), 543–51.

Flavell, J.H. and Draguns, J. "A Microgenetic Approach to Perception and Thought," *Psychological Bulletin*, 54 (1957), 197–217.

Ford, D.H., and Urban, H.B. *Systems of Psychotherapy: A Comparative Study.* New York, Wiley, 1963.

Foulkes, D. "Dream Reports from Different States of Sleep," *Journal of Abnormal and Social Psychology*, 65 (1962), 14–25.

Foulkes, D., and Vogel, G. "Mental Activity at Sleep Onset," *Journal of Abnormal and Social Psychology*, 70 (1965), 231–43.

Freud, S. *The Interpretation of Dreams.* Translated by J. Strachey. London, Allen and Unwin, 1954.

———. *Psychopathology of Everyday Life* (1901). Standard Edition, London, Hogarth, 1961.

———. *Notes upon a Case of Obsessional Neurosis* (1909). Standard Edition, Vol. 10. London, Hogarth, 1961.

———. *Psycho-analytic Notes on an Autobiographical Account of a Case of Paranoia (Dementia Paranoides)* (1911). Standard Edition, Vol. 12. London, Hogart, 1961.

———. *Repression* (1915). Standard Edition, Volume 14. London, Hogarth, 1961.

———. *Beyond the Pleasure Principle* (1920). Standard Edition, Vol. 18. London, Hogarth, 1961.

———. *Neuroses and Psychoses* (1924). Standard Edition, Vol. 19. London, Hogarth, 1961.

———. *Inhibition, Symptoms and Anxiety* (1926). Standard Edition, Vol. 20. London, Hogarth, 1961.

———. *Moses and Monotheism* (1939). Standard Edition, Vol. 23. London, Hogarth, 1961.

———. *An Outline of Psychoanalysis* (1940). Translated by J. Strachey. New York, W.W. Norton, 1949.

Galambos, R., in *Brain Mechanisms and Learning.* A symposium organized by C.I.O.M.C. Oxford, Blackwell, 1961.

Gamburg, A.L. "Orienting and Defensive Reactions in Simple and Paranoid Forms of Schizophrenia," in L.Y. Voromin, A.N. Leontiev, A.R. Luria, E.N. Sokolov, and O.S. Vinogradova. (eds.), *Orienting Reflex and Exploratory Behavior.* Washington, D.C., American Institute of Biological Sciences, 1965.

Gardner, R.A., and Gardner, B.T. "Teaching Sign Language to a Chimpanzee," *Science,* 165 (1969), 664–72.

Gardner, R., Holzman, P.S., Klein, G.S., Linton, H. and Spence, D.P. "Cognitive Control: A Study of Individual Characteristics in Cognitive Behavior," *Psychological Issues,* 1 (1959), 351–59.

Goldstein, L., Murphee, H.B., Sugerman, A.A., Pfeiffer, C.C. and Jenney, E.H. "Quantitative Electroencephalographic Analysis of Natural Occurring (Schizophrenia) and Drug Induced Psychotic States in Human Males," *Clin. Pharmacol. Ther.,* 4 (1963), 10–21.

Goldstein, L., Sugerman, A.A., Stolberg, H., Murphee, H.B., and Pfeiffer, C.C. "Electro-cerebral Activity in Schizophrenics and Non-Psychotic Subjects: Quantitative EEG Amplitude Analysis," *EEG and Clinical Neurophysiology,* 19 (1965), 350–61.

Goodenough, D.R., Shapiro, A., Holden, M., and Steinschriber, L. "A Comparison of 'Dreamers' and 'Non-dreamers'," *Journal of Abnormal and Social Psychology,* (1959), 295–302.

Goodman, T.Z. "Influence of Parental Figures on Schizophrenic Patients," *Journal of Abnormal Psychology,* 73 (1968), 503–72.

Goodwin, D.W., Powell, B., Bremer, D., Haskell, H., and Stern, J. "Alcohol and Recall: State-dependent Effects in Man," *Science,* 193 (1969), 1358–60.

Griesinger, W. *Pathologie und Therapie der psychischen Krankheiten.* Stuttgart, 1845.

Grinker, R.R., Miller, J., Sabshin, M., Nunn, R., and Nunnally, J.C. *The Phenomena of Depressions.* New York, Appleton-Century-Crofts, 1961.

Haidenhain, 1881, see Bubnoff, W., and Haidenhain, R. (1881).

Hall, C.S., and VanDeCastle, R.L. *The Content Analysis of Dreams.* New York, Appleton-Century-Crofts, 1966.

Hebb, D.O. *Organization of Behavior* (1949). New York, Science Editions, 1961.

Hebb, D.O., *A Textbook of Psychology.* Philadelphia, Saunders, 1966.

Hebbard, F.W., and Fischer, R.R. "Effect of Psylocybin, LSD and Mescaline on Small, Involuntary Eye Movements," *Psychopharmacologia,* 9 (1966), 146–56.

Hefferline, R.F., and Bruno, L.Y. "The Psychophysiology of Private Events," in O. Shapiro *et al.* (eds.), *Biofeedback and Self-Control.* Chicago, Aldine, 1972.

Herbart, J.F. *"Psychologie als Wissenschaft neu gegrundet auf Erfahrung, Metaphysik und Mathematik"* (1825), *Samtliche Werke* (ed. K. Kehrbach), Langensalra, 1892.

Hernandez-Peon, R. "Central Neuro-humoral Transmission in Sleep and Wakefulness," in K. Akert, C. Bally, and Y. Schade (eds.), *Progress in Brain Research*. Amsterdam, Elsevier, 1965.

Hersch, R.G., Antrobus, J.S., Arkin, A.M., and Singer, J.L. "Dreaming as a Function of Sympathetic Arousal," *Psychophysiology*, 7 (1970), 220–329.

Heston, R.R. and Denney, D. "Interactions between Life Experience and Biological Factors in Schizophrenia," in D. Rosenthal and S.S. Kety (eds.), *The Transmission of Schizophrenia*. London, Pergamon Press, 1968.

Hildebrandt, F.W. *Der Traum und seine Verwertung für's Leben*. Leipzig, 1875.

Hilgard, E.R., and Atkinson, R.C. *Introduction to Psychology*. New York, Harcourt, Brace and World, 1967.

Hobson, Y.A., Goldfrank, F., and Snyder, F. "Respiration and Mental Activity in Sleep," *Journal of Psychiatric Research*, 3 (1965), 79–90.

Holst, von E., und Mittelstaedt, H. "Das Reafferenz-problem," *Naturwissenschaften*, 37 (1950), 464–76. An abridged version appears in *Animal Behaviour*, 2 (1954) 89–94, reprinted in H.W. Leibowitz (ed.), *Visual Perception* New York, Macmillan, 1965.

Holt, R.R. "A Critical Examination of Freud's Concept of Bound vs. Free Cathexis," *Journal of American Psychoanalytic Association* (1963), 425–525.

Holzman, P.S., and Gardner, R.W. "Leveling and Sharpening," *Journal of Abnormal and Social Psychology*, 59 (1959), 151–55.

Holzman, P.S. and Gardner, R.W., "Leveling-Sharpening and Memory Organization," *Journal of Abnormal and Social Psychology*, 61 (1960), 176–80.

James, W. *The Principles of Psychology*. New York, Holt, 1890.

Janet, P. *Les obsessions et la psychasthenie*. Paris, Baillière, 1903.

Jasper, H.H., Fitzpatrick, C.P., and Solomon, P. "Analysis and Opposites in Schizophrenia and Epilepsy: Electroencephalographic and Clinical Studies," *American Journal of Psychiatry*, 95 (1939), 835–51.

Johnson, L. C. "A Psychophysiology for All States," *Psychophysiology*, 6 (1970), 501–16.

Johnson, N.F. "Chunking and Organization in the Process of Recall," in G. Bower (ed.), *The Psychology of Learning and Motivation*, Vol. 4. New York, Academic Press, 1970.

———. "Organization and the Concept of a Memory Code," in A.W. Melton and E. Martin (eds.), *Coding Processes in Human Memory*. Washington, D.C., Winston and Sons, 1972.

Bibliography 169

Kalmus, H., Fry, D.B., and Denes, P. "Effects of Delayed Visual Control on Writing, Drawing and Tracing," *Language and Speech*, 3 (1960), 96–108.

Kamiya, Y. "Conscious Control of Brain Waves," *Psychology Today*, 1 (1968), 57–60.

Kardiner, A., and Spiegel, H. *War Stress and Neurotic Illness*. New York, Hoeber, 1947.

Kimble, G.A. *Hilgard and Marquis' Conditioning and Learning*. New York, Appleton-Century-Crofts, 1961.

Klein, H. and Horwitz, W. "Psychological Factors in the Paranoid Phenomena," *American Journal of Psychiatry*, 105 (1949), 697–701.

Koch, S. *Psychology, A Study of Science*. New York, McGraw-Hill, 1959.

Köhler, W. *The Mentality of Apes* (1917). New York, Harcout, Brace and World, 1925.

Kohut, H. *The Analysis of the Self: A Systematic Approach to the Psychoanalytic Treatment of Narcissistic Personality Disorders*. New York, International Universities Press, 1971.

Kornetsky, C. and Mirsky, A.F. "On Certain Psychopharmalogical and Physiological Differences between Schizophrenic and Normal Persons," *Psychopharmacologia*, 8 (1966), 309–18.

Kramer, M., Winget, C. and Whitman, R.M. "A City Dreams: A Survey Approach to Normative Dream Content," *American Journal of Psychiatry*, 127 (1971), 1350–56.

Krech, D., Crutchfield, R.S., and Livson, N. *Elements of Psychology*. New York, Knopf, 1969.

Kris, E. *Psychoanalytic Explorations in Art*. New York, International Universities Press, 1952.

Lang, P.Y. "Autonomic Control, or Learning to Play the Internal Organs," *Psychology Today*, 4 (1970), 37–41.

Langfeldt, G. "Schizophrenia: Diagnosis and Prognosis," *Behavioral Science*, 14 (1969); also in R. Cancro (ed.), *The Schizophrenic Syndrome*. New York, Bruner/Mazel, 1971.

Lashley, K.S. "The Problem of Cerebral Organization in Vision," in H. Kluver (ed.), *Visual Mechanisms, Biological Symposia VII*. Lancaster, Pa., Jacques Cattel Press, 1942.

———. "The Problem of Serial Order in Behavior," in L.A. Jeffress (ed.), *Cerebral Mechanisms in Behavior, The Hixon Symposium*. New York, Wiley, 1951.

Lebedinskaya, E.J., Feigenberg, J.M., and Frierov, O.E. "Generalized Orientation Responses in the Defective Stage of Schizophrenia," *Soviet Psychology and Psychiatry*, 1 (1962), 51–57.

Lee, B.S. "Effects of Delayed Speech Feedback," *J. Acoust. Soc. Am.*, 22 (1950), 824–26.

———. "Artificial Stutter," *J. Speech Hear. Dis.*, 16 (1951), 53–55.

Lennox, W.G. *Epilepsy and Related Disorders*. Boston, Little Brown, 1960.

Lewis, A.J. *Inquiries in Psychiatry*. London, Routledge and Kegan Paul, 1967.

———. "Problems of Obsessional Illness," *Proceedings of the Royal Society of Medicine*, 29 (1935/36), 226–325.

Lindeman, E. "Psychological Changes in Normal and Abnormal Individuals under the Influence of Sodium Amytal," *American Journal of Psychiatry*, 71 (1932), 1083–91.

Lindsley, D.B. "The Reticular Formation and Perceptual Discrimination," in H.H. Jasper *et al.* (eds.), *Reticular Formation of the Brain*. London, Churchill.

Lorenz, K. *On Agression* (1963). London, Methuen, 1966.

Luborsky, L. "Momentary Forgetting During Psychotherapy and Psychoanalysis: A Theory and Research Method," in R.R. Holt (ed.), *Motives and Thought, Psychoanalytical Essays in Honor of D. Rapaport*. New York, International Universities Press, 1967.

Ludwig, A.M. "Altered States of Consciousness," *Archives of General Psychiatry*, 15 (1966), 225–34.

Luria, A.R. *The Human Brain and Psychic Processes*. New York, Harper, 1966.

MacDonald, N. "Living with Schizophrenia," *Canadian M.A.J.*, 82 (1960), 218.

MacKay, D.G. "Spoonerisms: The Structure of Errors in the Serial Order of Speech," *Neuropsychologia*, 8 (1970), 323–50.

Maier, N.R.F. *Frustration: The Study of Behaviour Without a Goal*. New York, McGraw-Hill, 1949.

———. "Frustration Theory: Restatement and Extension," *Psychological Review*, 63 (1956), 370–87.

Marmor, J. "Psychoanalytic Therapy as an Educational Process," in J. Masserman (ed.), *Science and Psychoanalysis*. New York, Grune and Stratton, 1962.

———. "Limitations of Free Association," *Archives of General Psychiatry*, 22 (1970), 160–65.

Marshal, J.C., and Newcombe, F. "Syntactic and Semantic Errors in Paralexia," *Neuropsychologia*, 9 (1966), 169–76.

Masserman, J.H. *Principles of Dynamic Psychiatry*. Sannolen, 1961.

———. "Anxiety: Aspects and Answers," in G.L. Usdin (ed.), *Psychoneurosis and Schizophrenia*. Philadelphia, Lippincott, 1966.

Meehl, P.E. "Schizotaxia, Schizotypy, Schizophrenia," *American Psychologist*, 1952.

Mellett, P.Y. "The Clinical Problem," in H.R. Beech (ed.), *Obsessional States*. London, Methuen, 1974.

Melzack, R. "Effects of Early Experience on Behavior: Experimental and Conceptual Considerations," in P.H. Hoch and J. Zubin (eds.), *Psychopathology of Perception*. New York, Grune and Stratton, 1965.

Meringer, R. and Mayer, K. *Versprechen und Verlesen: Eine psychologisch-linguistische Studie*. Stuttgart, 1895.

Merton, P.A. "Human Position Sense and Sense of Effort," in *Homeostasis and Feedback Mechanisms, Soc. Exp. Biol. Symp. XVIII*. London, Cambridge University Press, 1964.

Mészáros (1965). See Adam, G., *Interoception and Behaviour*. Budapest, Akademai Kiado, 1967.

McAdam, D.W., and Whitaker, H.A. "Language Production: Electroencephalographic Localization in the Normal Human Brain," *Science*, 172 (1971), 499–502.

McGhie, A. and Chapman, J. "Disorders of Attention and Perception in Early Schizophrenia," *British Journal of Medical Psychology*, 34 (1961), 103.

McLaughlin, R.J., and Eysenck, H.J. "Visual Masking as a Function of Personality," *British Journal of Psychiatry*, 57 (1966), 393–96.

McNeill, D. *The Acquisition of Language*. New York, Harper and Row, 1970.

Miller, G.A. "The Magical Number Seven, Plus or Minus Two: Some Limits of our Capacity for Processing Information," *Psychological Review*, 63 (1956), 81–97.

Miller, G.A., Galanter, E., and Pribram, K.H. *Plans and the Structure of Behavior*. New York, Holt Reinhart, 1960.

Miller, N.E. "Psychosomatic Effects of Specific Types of Training," *Annals of New York Academy of Sciences*, 159 (1969), 1025–40.

Moruzzi, G. "Active Process in the Brain Stem During Sleep," *The 1963 Harvey Lectures*, 588.

Moskowitz, F., and Berger, R.J. "Rapid Eye Movements and Dream Imagery —Are They Related?" *Nature*, 224 (1969), 613–14.

Muller, G.E., and Pilzecker, A. "Experimentelle Beitrage für Lehre vom Gedachtnis," *Zeitschrift für Psychologie*, 1900, Suppl. No. 1.

Neisser, U. *Cognitive Psychology*. New York, Appleton-Century-Crofts, 1966.

Nerval, Gerard de, *Aurelia*, ed. Jose Corti. Collection Romantique, 1956.

Nickerson, R.S. "The Effect of Preceding and Following Auditory Stimuli on Response Times to Visual Stimuli," *Acta Psychologica*, 33 (1970), 5–20.

Osgood, C.E., Suci, G.Y., and Tannenbaum, P.H. *The Measurement of Meaning.* Urbana, Illinois University Press, 1957.

Overton, D.A. "State-Dependent or 'Dissociated' Learning Produced with Pentobarbitol," *Journal of Comparative and Physiological Psychology,* 57 (1964), 3–12.

Ovesey, R. "Pseudohomosexuality, the Paranoid Mechanism, and Paranoia: An Adaptation Revision of a Classical Freudian Theory," *Psychiatry,* 18 (1955), 163–73.

Pavlov, J.P. *Conditioned Reflexes.* London, Oxford University Press, 1927.

Penfield, W. and Roberts, L. *Speech and Brain-Mechanisms.* Princeton, 1959.

Peper, E. "Localized, EEG Alpha Feedback Training: A Possible Technique for Mapping Subjective, Conscious, and Behavioral Experiences," in D. Shapiro *et al.* (eds.), *Biofeedback and Self-Control.* Chicago, Aldine, 1972.

Petrie, A. *Individuality in Pain and Suffering.* Chicago, University of Chicago Press, 1967

Piaget, J. *The Psychology of Intelligence,* (1947). New York, Harcourt, Brace, 1950.

———. *Play, Dreams, and Imitation,* (1946). New York, W.W. Norton, 1957.

Pivik, T. and Dement, W.C. "Phasic Changes in Muscular and Reflex Activity during non-REM Sleep," *Experimental Neurology,* 24 (1970), 115–24.

Plananski, K. and Johnston, T. "The Incidence and Relationship of Homosexual and Paranoid Features in Schizophrenia," *British Journal of Psychiatry,* 108 (1962), 604–15.

Poetzl, O. "Preconscious Stimulation in Dreams, Associations and Images," (1917), *Psychological Issues,* 2 (1960).

———. "The Relationship Between Experimentally Induced Dream Images and Indirect Vision" (1917), *Psychological Issues,* 2 (1960).

Pollin, W., and Stabenaw, J.R. "Biological, Psychological and Historical Differences in a Series of Monozygotic Twins Discordant for Schizophrenia," in D. Rosenthal and S.S. Kety (eds.), *The Transmission of Schizophrenia.* London, Pergamon Press, 1968.

Popper, N. *The Logic of Scientific Discovery.* New York, Science Edition, 1961.

Portmann, A. "Was bedeutet uns die lebendige Gestalt?" *Neue Sammlung,* 6 (1966), 1–7.

Powdermaker, F., Lewis, H.T., and Touraine, G. "Psychopathology and Treatment of Delinquent Girls," *American Journal of Orthopsychiatry,* 7 (1947), 58–71.

Premack, D. "Language in Chimpanzees," *Science,* 172 (1971), 808–22.

Pribram, K.H. *Languages of the Brain: Experimental Paradoxes and Principles in Neuropsychology.* New York, Prentice-Hall, 1971.

Rank, O. *The Myth of the Birth of the Hero and Other Writings,* (1936). Edited by P. Freund, New York, Vintage Books.

Rapaport, D. *Organization and Pathology of Thought.* New York, Columbia University Press, 1951.

Razran, G. "The Observable Unconscious and the Inferrable Conscious in Current Soviet Psychophysiology: Interoceptive Conditioning, Semantic Conditioning and the Orienting Reflex," *Psychological Review,* 68 (1961).

Redl, F. and Wineman, D. *Children Who Hate* (1951). New York, Free Press, 1965.

Reiff, P. and Scheerer, M. *Memory and Hypnotic Age Regression: Developmental Aspects of Cognitive Function Explored through Hypnosis,* New York, International Universities Press, 1959.

Richardson and Moore "On the Manifest Dream in Schizophrenia," *Journal of American Psychoanalytic Association,* 11 (1963), 281–302.

Robert, W. *Der Traum als Naturntowendigkeit erklärt.* 1886, Hamburg.

Ross, A.S.C., Clarke, R.F., and Hadock, N.L. "Edition of Text from a Dysphasic Patient," in A.S. DeRueck, and Maeve O'Connor (eds.), 298–317, *Disorders of Language, Ciba Foundation Symposium.* London, Churchill, 1964.

Sander, F. "Experimentelle Ergebnisse der Gestaltpsychologie," in E. Becker (ed.), *10 Kongress Ber. Exp. Psychol.* Jena, Fischer, 1928.

———. "Structure, Totality of Experience, and Gestalt," in C. Murchison (ed.), *Psychologies of 1930.* Worcester, Clark University Press, 1930.

Schachtel, E. "On Memory and Childhood Amnesia," *Psychiatry,* 10 (1947), 1–26.

Schachter, S., and Singer, T.E. "Cognitive, Social and Physiological Determinants of Emotional State," *Psychological Review,* 69 (1962), 379–97.

Scherner, K.A. *Das Leben des Traumes.* Berlin, 1861.

Scheler, M. *Die Stellung des Menschen in Kosmos.* Darmstadt, O. Reichler, 1927.

Schilder, P. "On the Development of Thoughts" (1920), in D. Rapaport (ed.), *Organization and Pathology of Thought.* New York, Columbia University Press, 1951.

Schooler C., and Zahn, T.P. "The Effect of Closeness of Social Interaction on Task Performance and Arousal in Chronic Schizophrenia," *Journal of Nervous and Mental Diseases,* 147 (1968), 397–401.

Schur, M. "Comments on the Metapyschology of Somatization," *The Psychoanalytic Study of the Child,* 10 (1955), 119–64.

Shagass, C. "A Neurophysiological Approach to Perceptual Psychopathology," in P.H. Hoch, and J. Zubin (eds.), *Psychopathology of Perception*. New York, Grune and Stratton, 1965.

Shagass, C., and Schwartz, M. "Cerebral Responsiveness Found in Psychiatric Patients," *Archives of General Psychiatry*, 8 (1963), 177–89.

Shevrin, H., and Luborsky, L. "The Measurement of Preconscious Perception in Dreams and Images: An Investigation of the Poetzl Phenomenon," *Journal of Abnormal and Social Psychology*, 56 (1958), 285–94.

Silberer, H. "On Symbol-Formation," (1912), in D. Rapaport (ed.), *Organization and Pathology of Thought*. New York, Columbia University Press, 1951.

Silverman, J.A. "A Paradigm for the Study of Altered States of Consciousness," *British Journal of Psychiatry*, 114 (1968), 1200–18.

Snyder, F. "The Physiology of Dreaming," in M. Kramer (ed.), *Dream Psychology and the New Biology of Dreaming*. Springfield, Ill., Thomas, 1969.

Sokolov, Y.N. "Orienting Reflex as Information Regulator," in A. Leontyev, A. Luriya, and A. Smirov (eds.), *Psychological Research in the U.S.S.R.*, 1 (1966), 334–60.

Sperling, G. "Short-term Memory and Scanning in the Processing of Visual Information," in F.A. Young, and D.B. Lindsley (eds.), *Early Experience and Visual Information Processing*. Washington, D.C., National Academy of Science, 1970.

Sperry, R.W. "Hemisphere Deconnection and Unity in Conscious Awareness," *American Psychologist*, 23 (1968), 723–33.

Stevens, J.M. and Derbyshire, A.J. "Shift along the Alert-response Continuum during Remission of Catatonic Stupor with Amobarbital," *Psychosomatic Medicine*, 20 (1958), 99–107.

Svyadoshch, A. "The Assimilation and Memorization of Speech during Natural Sleep," in F. Rubin (ed.), *Current Research in Hypnoedia*. London, Macdonald, 1968.

Szasz, T.S. *The Myth of Mental Illness*. New York, Dell, 1961.

Stransky, E. *Uber Sprachverwirrtheit*. Marhold, Halle, 1905.

Sutton, S., and Zubin, J. "Effect of Sequence on Reaction Time in Schizophrenia," in A.T. Wilford, and J.E. Birch (eds.), *Behavior, Aging, and the Nervous System*. Springfield, Thomas, 1961.

Taylor, D.W. "Toward an Information Processing Theory of Motivation," in M.R. Jones (ed.), *Nebraska Symposium on Motivation*, 8 (1960), 51–79.

Teichner, W.H. "Recent Studies of Simple Reaction Time," *Psychological Bulletin*, 51 (1974), 128–49.

Teitelbaum, I. "Psychogenic Body Image Disturbances Associated with Psychogenic Aphasia and Agnosia," *Journal of Nervous and Mental Diseases*, 95 (1941), 581–612.

Tomkins, S.S. *Affect, Imagery and Consciousness.* New York, Springer, 1962.

Undeutsch, H. "Die Aktualgenese und ihrer Characterologischen Bedeutung," *Scientia,* 1942.

Urbantschitsch, V. *Uber Subjektive Horerscheinungen und Subjektive Optische Anschauungsbilder.* Leipzig, Deuticke, 1908.

Venables, P.H. "Psychophysiological Aspects of Schizophrenia," *British Journal of Medical Psychology,* 39 (1966), 289–97.

Venables, P.H., and Wing, J.K. "Level of Arousal and the Subclassification of Schizophrenia," *Archives of General Psychiatry,* 7 (1962), 114–19.

Walker, E.R. "Action Decrement and its Relation to Learning," *Psychological Review,* 65 (1958), 129–42.

Walker, E.R. and Tarte, R.D. "Memory Storage as a Function of Arousal and Time with Homogeneous and Heterogeneous Lists," *Journal of Verbal Learning and Verbal Behavior,* 2 (1963), 113–19.

Weckowicz, T.E., and Blewett, D.B. "Size Constancy and Abstract Thinking in Schizophrenic Patients," *Journal of Mental Science,* 105 (1959), 441.

Weiss, T. and Engel, B.T. "Operant Conditioning of Heart Rate in Patients with Premature Ventricular Contractions," *Psychosomatic Medicine,* 33 (1971), 301–21.

Werner, H. "Microgenesis and Aphasia," *Journal of Abnormal and Social Psychology,* 52 (1959), 347–53.

Westphal, C. "Zwangsvorstellungen," *Archiv für Psychiatrie und Nervenkunde,* 8 (1878), 734–50.

Wickens, D.D. "Encoding Characteristics of Words: An Empirical Approach to Meaning," *Psychological Review,* 76 (1969), 559–73.

Voronin and Guselnikov (1963), quoted in S.H. Birch, and A. Lefford, "Visual Differentiation, Intersensory Integration, and Voluntary Motor Control," *Monographs of the Society for Research in Child Development,* Vol. 32, 1967.

Wolff, R.H. "Cognitive Considerations for a Psychoanalytic Theory of Language Acquisition," in R.R. Holt (ed.), *Motives and Thought, Psychoanalytic Essays in Honor of D. Rapaport.* New York, Columbia University Press, 1967.

Yates, A.Y. "Delayed Auditory Feedback," *Psychological Bulletin,* 60 (1961), 213–32.

Zimmerman, W. *Psychological and Physiological Differences between "Light" and "Deep" Sleepers.* Unpublished dissertation, University of Chicago, 1967.

AUTHOR INDEX

SUBJECT INDEX

Korsakov's disease 51, 142

Language, 115
Levellers, 25
Libido, 9, 10, 35
Limen, 53

Masking effect, 23
Maudsley Personality Inventory, 22
Memory code, 129
Me–ness, 143
Mental apparatus, 83
Mental health, 6–8
Microgenesis, 59–67
Motor dysfunctions, 28

Neurosis, 74–79, 81

Oedipus complex, 40

Pain, 21, 22
Pathogenesis, 4
Perceiving, 57
Phobia, 38
Pleasure principle, 78, 79
Primary processes, 49–58
Psychical censorship 83, 84
Psychical locality, 5
Psychoanalytic psychology, 76, 83
Psychodynamics, 1, 20
Psychopathology, 17, 6, 150–162
Psychopathy, 138–149
Psychosomatic, 11, 12, 32
Punishment, 83, 84
PVC, 33

Reaction time, 119
Reafference, 123
Recall, 48
Reflexes, 14
Regression, 71, 126
Remembering, 57
Repression, 24, 43–48

Schematizing test, 25, 26
Schizophrenia, 51, 99, 108–137
Secondary processes, 49–58
Self-actualization, 7, 8
Sensory deprivation, 18–20, 56
Sleep, 101
    deep, 101
    light, 101
    system, 103
Slips of the tongue, 3
Social interaction, 88
Stimulation, 18
Superego, 49, 90

Test-Operate-Test-Exit, 154
Thematic Apperception Test, 87
Therapeutic intervention, 11
Transfer, 16, 48

Unattended-to inputs, 93–97

Vigilance system, 103

Weber-Fechner's law, 53

Wish-fulfillment theory, 89
Word Association Test, 125